Manhattan Review

Test Prep & Admissions Consulting

Turbocharge Your GMAT
Math Study Companion

5th Edition (December 18th, 2012)

- ☐ *Complete & Challenging Training Sets*
  - · *Problem Solving - 140+ Questions*
  - · *Data Sufficiency - 120+ Questions*
- ☐ *Comprehensive Solutions*
- ☐ *Graphic Illustrations*
- ☐ *Quick Answer Keys*
- ☐ *Training Set Question List by Concept*
- ☐ *Free Web Downloads Available*

www.manhattanreview.com

Copyright and Terms of Use

Copyright and Trademark

All materials herein (including names, terms, trademarks, designs, images and graphics) are the property of Manhattan Review, except where otherwise noted. Except as permitted herein, no such material may be copied, reproduced, displayed or transmitted or otherwise used without the prior written permission of Manhattan Review. You are permitted to use material herein for your personal, non-commercial use, provided that you do not combine such material into a combination, collection or compilation of material. If you have any questions regarding the use of the material, please contact Manhattan Review at info@manhattanreview.com.

This material may make reference to countries and persons. The use of such references is for hypothetical and demonstrative purposes only.

Terms of Use

By using this material, you acknowledge and agree to the terms of use contained herein.

No Warranties

This material is provided without warranty, either express or implied, including the implied warranties of merchantability, of fitness for a particular purpose and non-infringement. Manhattan Review does not warrant or make any representations regarding the use, accuracy or results of the use of this material. This material may make reference to other source materials. Manhattan Review is not responsible in any respect for the content of such other source materials, and disclaims all warranties and liabilities with respect to the other source materials.

Limitation on Liability

Manhattan Review shall not be responsible under any circumstances for any direct, indirect, special, punitive or consequential damages ("Damages") that may arise from the use of this material. In addition, Manhattan Review does not guarantee the accuracy or completeness of its course materials, which are provided "as is" with no warranty, express or implied. Manhattan Review assumes no liability for any Damages from errors or omissions in the material, whether arising in contract, tort or otherwise.

GMAT is a registered trademark of the Graduate Management Admission Council.
GMAC does not endorse nor is it affiliated in any way with the owner of this product or any content herein.

10-Digit International Standard Book Number: (ISBN: 1629260142)
13-Digit International Standard Book Number: (ISBN: 978-1-62926-014-3)

Last updated on December 18, 2012.

Manhattan Review, 275 Madison Avenue, Suite 424, New York, NY 10025.
Phone: +1 (212) 316-2000. E-Mail: info@manhattanreview.com. Web: www.manhattanreview.com

About the Turbocharge your GMAT Series [5th Edition]

The highly acclaimed Turbocharge Your GMAT series is the result of the arduous effort of Manhattan Review to offer the most comprehensive and clear treatment of the concepts tested in the GMAT. The Manhattan Review Turbocharge Your GMAT preparation materials include over 600 pages of well-illustrated and professionally presented strategies and originally written problems for both the Verbal Section and Quantitative Section, 200 pages of detailed solutions, and more than 300 pages of internally developed Quantitative Glossary and Verbal Vocabulary List with detailed definitions, related words and sentence examples. The detailed breakdown of exclusive practice problems per category is 40+ Reading Comprehension passages, 60 Critical Reasoning questions, 250 Sentence Correction questions, and 300+ Quantitative questions.
Manhattan Review uses this material when delivering its weekend crash courses, one-week intensive courses, weekday and weekend long courses, online workshops, free seminars, and private tutoring to students in the US, UK, Continental Europe, Asia and the rest of the world. Please visit www.manhattanreview.com to find out more and also take a free GMAT practice test!

- ☐ GMAT Math Study Guide (ISBN: 978-1-62926-013-6)
- ■ GMAT Math Study Companion (ISBN: 978-1-62926-014-3)
- ☐ GMAT Verbal Study Guide (ISBN: 978-1-62926-015-0)
- ☐ GMAT Verbal Study Companion (ISBN: 978-1-62926-016-7)
- ☐ GMAT Math Essentials (ISBN: 978-1-62926-017-4)
- ☐ GMAT Algebra (ISBN: 978-1-62926-018-1)
- ☐ GMAT Geometry (ISBN: 978-1-62926-019-8)
- ☐ GMAT Word Problems & Statistics (ISBN: 978-1-62926-020-4)
- ☐ GMAT Combinatorics & Probability (ISBN: 978-1-62926-021-1)
- ☐ GMAT Sentence Correction Guide (ISBN: 978-1-62926-022-8)
- ☐ GMAT Critical Reasoning Guide (ISBN: 978-1-62926-023-5)
- ☐ GMAT Reading Comprehension Guide (ISBN: 978-1-62926-024-2)
- ☐ GMAT Integrated Reasoning Guide (ISBN: 978-1-62926-025-9)
- ☐ GMAT Vocabulary Builder (ISBN: 978-1-62926-026-6)

About the Company

Manhattan Review's origin can be traced directly to an Ivy-League MBA classroom in 1999. While lecturing on advanced quantitative subjects to MBAs at Columbia Business School in New York City, Prof. Dr. Joern Meissner was asked by his students to assist their friends, who were frustrated with conventional GMAT preparation options. He started to create original lectures that focused on presenting the GMAT content in a coherent and concise manner rather than a download of voluminous basic knowledge interspersed with so-called "tricks." The new approach immediately proved highly popular with GMAT students, inspiring the birth of Manhattan Review. Over the past 15+ years, Manhattan Review has grown into a multi-national firm, focusing on GMAT, GRE, LSAT, SAT, and TOEFL test prep and tutoring, along with business school, graduate school and college admissions consulting, application advisory and essay editing services.

About the Founder

Professor Joern Meissner, the founder and chairman of Manhattan Review has over twenty-five years of teaching experience in undergraduate and graduate programs at prestigious business schools in the USA, UK and Germany. He created the original lectures, which are constantly updated by the Manhattan Review Team to reflect the evolving nature of the GMAT GRE, LSAT, SAT, and TOEFL test prep and private tutoring. Professor Meissner received his Ph.D. in Management Science from Graduate School of Business at Columbia University (Columbia Business School) in New York City and is a recognized authority in the area of Supply Chain Management (SCM), Dynamic Pricing and Revenue Management. Currently, he holds the position of Full Professor of Supply Chain Management and Pricing Strategy at Kuehne Logistics University in Hamburg, Germany. Professor Meissner is a passionate and enthusiastic teacher. He believes that grasping an idea is only half of the fun; conveying it to others makes it whole. At his previous position at Lancaster University Management School, he taught the MBA Core course in Operations Management and originated three new MBA Electives: Advanced Decision Models, Supply Chain Management, and Revenue Management. He has also lectured at the University of Hamburg, the Leipzig Graduate School of Management (HHL), and the University of Mannheim. Professor Meissner offers a variety of Executive Education courses aimed at business professionals, managers, leaders, and executives who strive for professional and personal growth. He frequently advises companies ranging from Fortune 500 companies to emerging start-ups on various issues related to his research expertise. Please visit his academic homepage www.meiss.com for further information.

Manhattan Review Advantages

▶ **Time Efficiency and Cost Effectiveness**

   – The most limiting factor in test preparation for most people is time.

   – It takes significantly more teaching experience and techniques to prepare a student in less time.

   – Our preparation is tailored for busy professionals. We will teach you what you need to know in the least amount of time.

▶ **High-quality and dedicated instructors who are committed to helping every student reach her/his goals**

▶ **Manhattan Review's team members have combined wisdom of**

   – Academic achievements

   – MBA teaching experience at prestigious business schools in the US and UK

   – Career success

▶ **Our curriculum & proprietary Turbocharge Your GMAT course materials**

   – About 600 pages of well-illustrated and professionally presented strategies and exclusive problems for both the Verbal and the Quantitative Sections

   – 200+ pages of detailed solutions

   – 300-page of internally developed Quantitative and Verbal vocabulary list with detailed definitions, related words and sentence examples

   – Challenging Online CATs (Included in any course payments; Available for separate purchases)

▶ **Combine with Private Tutoring for an individually tailored study package**

▶ **Special Offer for Our Online Recording Library (Visit Online Library on our website)**

▶ **High-quality Career, MBA & College Advisory Full Service**

▶ **Our Pursuit of Excellence in All Areas of Our Service**

Visit us often at www.ManhattanReview.com.
(Select International Locations for your local content!)

International Phone Numbers & Official Manhattan Review Websites

Manhattan Headquarters	+1-212-316-2000	www.manhattanreview.com
USA & Canada	+1-800-246-4600	www.manhattanreview.com
Australia	+61-3-9001-6618	www.manhattanreview.com
Austria	+43-720-115-549	www.review.at
Belgium	+32-2-808-5163	www.manhattanreview.be
China	+86-20-2910-1913	www.manhattanreview.cn
Czech Republic	+1-212-316-2000	www.review.cz
France	+33-1-8488-4204	www.review.fr
Germany	+49-89-3803-8856	www.review.de
Greece	+1-212-316-2000	www.review.com.gr
Hong Kong	+852-5808-2704	www.review.hk
Hungary	+1-212-316-2000	www.review.co.hu
India	+1-212-316-2000	www.review.in
Indonesia	+1-212-316-2000	www.manhattanreview.com
Ireland	+1-212-316-2000	www.gmat.ie
Italy	+39-06-9338-7617	www.manhattanreview.it
Japan	+81-3-4589-5125	www.manhattanreview.jp
Malaysia	+1-212-316-2000	www.manhattanreview.com
Netherlands	+31-20-808-4399	www.manhattanreview.nl
Philippines	+1-212-316-2000	www.review.ph
Poland	+1-212-316-2000	www.review.pl
Portugal	+1-212-316-2000	www.review.pt
Russia	+1-212-316-2000	www.manhattanreview.ru
Singapore	+65-3158-2571	www.gmat.sg
South Africa	+1-212-316-2000	www.manhattanreview.co.za
South Korea	+1-212-316-2000	www.manhattanreview.kr
Sweden	+1-212-316-2000	www.gmat.se
Spain	+34-911-876-504	www.review.es
Switzerland	+41-435-080-991	www.review.ch
Taiwan	+1-212-316-2000	www.gmat.tw
Thailand	+66-6-0003-5529	www.manhattanreview.com
United Arab Emirates	+1-212-316-2000	www.manhattanreview.ae
United Kingdom	+44-20-7060-9800	www.manhattanreview.co.uk
Rest of World	+1-212-316-2000	www.manhattanreview.com

Contents

Chapter 1

Math Training Set – Problem Solving

1. 10.8 grams of a certain chemical make only 9 percent of the total yield of a chemical reaction. If a lab technician observes 13.5 grams of this chemical, what percent of the total yield does it make?

   (A) 10.80%

   (B) 11.10%

   (C) 11.25%

   (D) 11.50%

   (E) 11.70%

2. Each new driving offense results in increasing penalty points per offense on a driver's 'rap sheet'. A driver gets one point for the first offense, and the incremental increase in penalty points for each new offense is 2 points. If the maximum number of offense points before the revocation of the license is 100, what is the maximum number of offenses a driver can make and continue to drive legally?

   (A) 8

   (B) 9

   (C) 10

   (D) 11

   (E) 12

3. An investor bought shares of stock for $75 per share and later sold his shares for $30. What was the percent change in the share price?

   (A) 150%

   (B) −60%

   (C) −75%

   (D) −150%

   (E) −250%

4. What is the value of $(u-1)^3$ if $u = \frac{6}{7} + \frac{18}{21} - \frac{12}{14}$?

   (A) $-\dfrac{1}{343}$

   (B) $-\dfrac{1}{7}$

   (C) $\dfrac{1}{7}$

(D) $\dfrac{27}{343}$

(E) $\dfrac{216}{343}$

5. The value of v is given by the formula $v = 13u$. If u is an integer greater than 35 and less than 41, then which of the following is the value of v?

(A) 533

(B) 520

(C) 480

(D) 455

(E) 440

6. The population of Country S is 10 million people less than the population of Country J. If in 5 years, Country J has twice as many people as Country S, how many people will live in Country S in three years given that each country has a constant population growth of 0.5 million people per year?

(A) 6

(B) 7.5

(C) 9

(D) 10.5

(E) 12

7. The value of the product of u and v is equal to twenty times the ratio of the value obtained by subtracting v from u to the value of v. If v equals 4, what is the value of u?

(A) 50

(B) 25

(C) 20

(D) 10

(E) 5

8. The relationship between quantities m and n is expressed by the equation $11m = 5(n - 42)$. If the difference between the two chosen values of n is 30, what is the difference in the corresponding values of m?

   (A) $\dfrac{30}{11}$

   (B) $\dfrac{42}{11}$

   (C) $\dfrac{60}{11}$

   (D) $\dfrac{150}{11}$

   (E) 14

9. How many factors of 80 are greater than $\sqrt{80}$?

   (A) Ten

   (B) Eight

   (C) Six

   (D) Five

   (E) Four

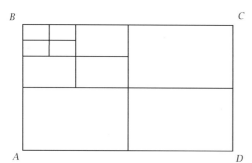

10. Rectangular region $ABCD$ shown above is partitioned into four identical smaller rectangular regions. Then similar partitioning is performed twice. If the smallest rectangular region thus obtained has the area equal to x, what is the total area of $ABCD$ in terms of x?

   (A) $16x$

   (B) $32x$

   (C) $40x$

   (D) $64x$

   (E) $12x$.

11. Which of the following can be odd?

I. The sum of 7 consecutive integers

II. The sum of 10 consecutive integers

III. The product of 13 consecutive integers

   (A) II only

   (B) I and II only

   (C) I and III only

   (D) II and III only

   (E) I, II, and III

12. How many three-digit numbers begin with a digit which represents an odd number that is a prime, have a prime number as a second digit, and end with a digit that represents an odd number?

   (A) 15

   (B) 60

   (C) 75

   (D) 80

   (E) 100

13. If $N = \frac{S}{1-pq}$ and $N, S, p,$ and q are positive numbers, then in terms of $N, S,$ and q what does p equal?

   (A) $\dfrac{N-S}{Nq}$

   (B) $1 - \dfrac{S}{Nq}$

   (C) $\dfrac{N-S}{q}$

   (D) $\dfrac{N}{S} - q$

   (E) $1 - \dfrac{Nq}{S}$

14.
$$
\begin{array}{r}
9\,6\,5 \\
7 \star 7 \\
+\,6 \star 3 \\
\hline
2,3 \star 5
\end{array}
$$

In the addition above, the number $\star$ must be

(A) 2

(B) 3

(C) 4

(D) 5

(E) 6

15. If $x > 0$ and $y < 0$, which of the following IS necessarily true?

(A) $x^2 + y^3 < 0$

(B) $x^5 < y^2$

(C) $x^2 + y^7 > 0$

(D) $y^2 + x > 0$

(E) $\dfrac{y^5}{x} > 0$

16. Jack, Tom, Beth, and Ruth are each competing to paint one side of a square fence. The fastest, Jack, painted his side in 13 hours, the slowest, Tom, painted his side in 14 hours. Which of the following could NOT be the average of the times that each of the four competitors spent painting his or her side of the fence?

(A) 13.2

(B) 13.3

(C) 13.5

(D) 13.6

(E) 13.7

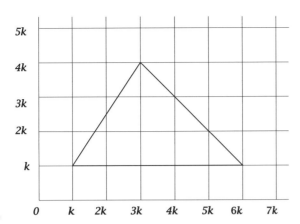

17.

If the area of the triangle above is 35, what is the value of k?

(A) $\sqrt{2}$

(B) $\frac{1}{3}\sqrt{21}$

(C) $\sqrt{3}$

(D) $\frac{1}{3}\sqrt{42}$

(E) $\sqrt{15}$

18. Oil revenue in the amount of x million dollars, x being an even number, is divided among 11 Russian oligarchs, giving each a fixed sum plus a remainder of 10 million for the government. Which of the following, when added to x, produces the sum which is divisible by 22?

(A) 3

(B) 5

(C) 7

(D) 12

(E) 17

19. Three consecutive numbers are drawn from integers, which are strictly greater than 9 and strictly less than 20. Suppose w is the product of the numbers drawn, which of the following must be true?

I. w is an integer multiple of 3.

II. w is an integer multiple of 4.

III. w is an integer multiple of 6.

(A) I only

    (B) II only

    (C) I and III only

    (D) II and III only

    (E) I, II, and III

20. The ratio of South Korean aircraft to North Korean aircraft was 1 to 3. After the North announced it would acquire nuclear weapons, the U.S. transferred 60 aircraft to South Korea. Then, the ratio became 3 to 5. What was the total number of the aircraft on the Korean peninsula after the U.S. aircraft transfer?

    (A) 120

    (B) 135

    (C) 225

    (D) 300

    (E) 360

21. A distributor sells a product through an on-line store, which takes a commission of 20 percent off the price set by the distributor. The distributor obtains the product from a producer at the price of 15 dollars per item. What is the price that a buyer observes on-line if the distributor wants to maintain a 20 percent profit on the cost of the item?

    (A) $18.00

    (B) $18.50

    (C) $22.00

    (D) $22.50

    (E) $27.00

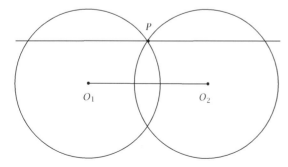

22.

In the figure above, two circles with radii equal to 10 units of length overlap such that their centres, O_1 and O_2, are 16 units apart. What is the distance between the line joining the centres of the circles and the line drawn through point P parallel to the line connecting the centres?

(A) 3

(B) 5

(C) 6

(D) 8

(E) 10

23. Admission to a certain ballet school is very competitive. $\frac{3}{8}$ of all applicants are male. $\frac{3}{4}$ of all applicants are rejected in the first round including $\frac{2}{3}$ of all male applicants. What fraction of applicants remaining after the first round are male?

(A) $\dfrac{1}{32}$

(B) $\dfrac{1}{4}$

(C) $\dfrac{1}{2}$

(D) $\dfrac{3}{4}$

(E) $\dfrac{8}{9}$

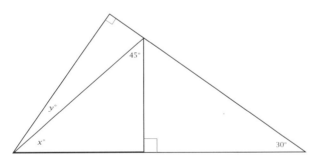

24.   Note: Figure not drawn to scale

In the figure above, what is the value of $2x - y$? x and y are denoted as the degree of corresponding angles.

(A) 15

(B) 30

(C) 45

(D) 60

(E) 75

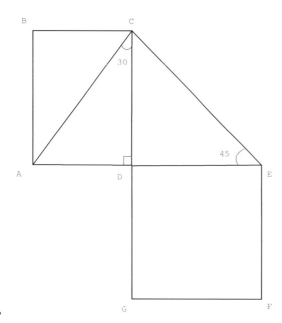

25.

If the area of rectangle $ABCD$ is $4\sqrt{3}$, then what is the area of the square $DEFG$?

(A) $\sqrt{3}$

(B) $2\sqrt{3}$

(C) 4

(D) $4\sqrt{3}$

(E) 12

26. $\dfrac{1}{\dfrac{3}{4} - \dfrac{2}{3}} =$

(A) $\dfrac{2}{7}$

(B) $\dfrac{3}{4}$

(C) $\dfrac{12}{5}$

(D) 5

(E) 12

27. The total distance between points A and C through point B along straight lines between each point is 150 kilometers. If the stretch between A and B is five times longer than that between B and C, what is the distance between points B and C?

(A) 32

(B) 30

(C) 28

(D) 25

(E) 24

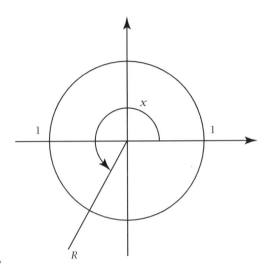

28.

Ray R starts its counter-clockwise revolution around the origin from the point $(1, 0)$ in a coordinate graph. After it travels for one full revolution and an additional angle of x, it stops at the above-illustrated position in the third quadrant. Let D denote the total distance traveled by the original point of $(0, 1)$ on ray R. What statements about D are true?

I. $\frac{5\pi}{4} < D < \frac{3\pi}{2}$

II. $-\pi < -D < -\frac{\pi}{2}$

III. $\frac{13\pi}{4} < D < \frac{7\pi}{2}$

(A) I only

(B) II only

(C) III only

(D) I and II only

(E) I and III only

29. A university professor received a government grant of M dollars to be spent on research during the year. 25 percent of the grant was appropriated by the university, so the professor used 20 percent of what was left to buy lab equipment. What percent of the original sum of M dollars was either given to the university or spent on lab equipment?

(A) 25%

(B) 40%

(C) 45%

(D) 47%

(E) 50%

30. Flying at constant speed, an airplane of type *I* (plane *I*) covers a certain distance between two points in 15 hours. An airplane of type *II* (plane *II*) covers the same distance in 10 hours. If plane *I* makes a landing after flying for 9 hours along the route, how many hours will it take plane *II* to complete the remainder of the route between the landing point of plane *I* and the destination?

(A) $\frac{2}{5}$

(B) $\frac{3}{5}$

(C) 2

(D) 3

(E) 4

31. Gaby, Dimitri, and Marat played a game of poker. At the end of the game, Gaby had 12 dollars more than Dimitri, but only one-half of what Marat had. If each player brought 20 dollars to the game, what were Gaby's total dollar winnings?

(A) −6

(B) −2

(C) 6

(D) 18

(E) 24

32. A certain retailer gets a shipment of items the day after his inventory drops below $\frac{y}{4}$ items. Each shipment replenishes the retailer's inventory up to the level y, and it is estimated that the retailer, on average, maintains $\frac{y}{2}$ in inventory every month throughout the year. The cost of keeping an item in inventory is \$0.5 per month. What is the retailer's annual inventory cost.

(A) $6y$

(B) $3y$

(C) $\dfrac{3y}{2}$

(D) $\dfrac{y}{2}$

(E) $\dfrac{y}{12}$

33. If $w = \dfrac{1 + \dfrac{xy}{z^2}}{x + y}, x = \dfrac{z}{2}$, and $y = \dfrac{3z}{4}$,

what is the value of w in terms of z?

(A) $\dfrac{11}{10z}$

(B) $\dfrac{2}{5z}$

(C) $\dfrac{3}{10z}$

(D) $\dfrac{11z}{10}$

(E) $\dfrac{2z}{5}$

34. If $y^2 = 195$, which of the following would be closest to a possible value of y?

   (A) -14

   (B) 19

   (C) 51

   (D) 97

   (E) $3,610$

35. A factory worker produced one lot of connecting clips, and initial quality control found that $\frac{5}{7}$ of clips in the lot could be used. An assembly plant purchased this lot of clips valuing the lot at $3 per each usable clip. During assembly, it became known that only $\frac{3}{5}$ of the clips in the lot were usable. What was price per usable clip that the assembly plant paid for the lot?

   (A) $\$2\dfrac{1}{7}$

   (B) $\$3\dfrac{4}{7}$

   (C) $\$5\dfrac{1}{4}$

   (D) $\$5$

   (E) $\$6\dfrac{3}{8}$

36. To enhance the performance of her PC, Marie-Ann purchased n megabytes of Random Access Memory (RAM). Soon thereafter, the price of memory decreased by $1.25 per megabyte. How much RAM in megabytes did Marie-Ann purchase if it became known that she could have saved $62.50, had she postponed her purchase for a short while?

(A) 25

(B) 50

(C) 75

(D) 100

(E) 125

37. If $x = 36$ and $n = 3$, then $\left(\frac{1}{x}\right)^{\frac{1}{n-1}} - \left(\frac{1}{x - n^{n-1}}\right)^{\frac{1}{n}} =$

(A) 1

(B) $\dfrac{1}{27}$

(C) $-\dfrac{1}{6}$

(D) $-\dfrac{1}{3}$

(E) $-\dfrac{1}{2}$

38. A group of tourists needed to walk 45 miles. During the first day the group walked 19 miles. To complete the required distance during the second day, the group had to cover the distance which was approximately what percent greater than the distance walked during the first day?

(A) 11%

(B) 16%

(C) 27%

(D) 37%

(E) 58%

39. If a is an integer divisible by 3, and b is not divisible by 3, which of the following is NOT divisible by 3?

(A) $a(b - 3)$

(B) $ab + 3$

   (C) $3(a + b)$

   (D) $3a + b$

   (E) $a + 3b$

40. Find an expression equivalent to the one below

$$\frac{(0.3667)(0.8333)(0.3333)}{(0.4444)(0.6667)(0.125)}.$$

   (A) 2.00

   (B) 2.40

   (C) 2.45

   (D) 2.75

   (E) 2.80

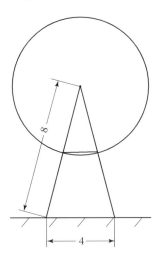

41. A model of London's Millennium Wheel in the cubicle of Manhattan Review's CEO has supports which are 4 centimeters apart, and a reinforcement bar of 2 centimeters in length. The length of each support is 8 centimeters. If a fly sits on top of the wheel, how high does it sit above the surface on which the supports rest?

   (A) $4\sqrt{3}$ cm

   (B) $2\sqrt{15}$ cm

   (C) $2 + 2\sqrt{15}$ cm

   (D) $4 + \sqrt{15}$ cm

   (E) $2(2 + \sqrt{15})$ cm

42. A budget airline charges each customer $e/3$ euros for every leg of the flights between London and Ibiza. The only exception is that it charges e euros for the first leg of the first round-trip for the same customer. How much is the total cost of n round-trip tickets for one customer?

   (A) $\dfrac{e + ne}{27}$

   (B) $\dfrac{2e + 2ne}{3}$

   (C) $\dfrac{2e + ne}{300}$

   (D) $\dfrac{2e + ne}{3}$

   (E) $\dfrac{ne}{9}$

43. If $uvw \neq 0$, and u percent of v percent of w is k, then w –

   (A) $\dfrac{100k}{uv}$

   (B) $\dfrac{1,000k}{uv}$

   (C) $\dfrac{10,000k}{uv}$

   (D) $\dfrac{uv}{10,000k}$

   (E) $\dfrac{10,000uv}{k}$

44. If u, v and w are single-digit integers and $1,000(u) + 10,000(v) + 10(w) = N$, what is the tens digit of the number N?

   (A) 0

   (B) 1

   (C) u

   (D) v

   (E) w

45. If the water level rises 20 percent from m meters to 12 meters, then $12 - m =$?

   (A) 2

   (B) 3

   (C) 7

   (D) 10

   (E) 25

46. $\sqrt{\dfrac{1}{36} + \dfrac{1}{64}} =$

(A) $\dfrac{1}{12}$

(B) $\dfrac{1}{7}$

(C) $\dfrac{1}{10}$

(D) $\dfrac{5}{24}$

(E) $\dfrac{7}{24}$

47. To keep the structural integrity of a mechanical system, the horizontal co-ordinate x may be any number, whereas it vertical co-ordinate y must be such that its third power is less than or equal to the numerical value of x. Each of the following pairs satisfies this rule EXCEPT

(A) $(125, 5)$

(B) $(85, 3)$

(C) $(57, 4)$

(D) $(1, 1)$

(E) $(1, 0)$

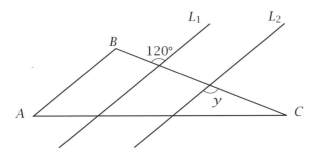

48.

In $\triangle ABC$ above, $AB \| L_1$. What is the measure of angle y?

(A) 80

(B) 90

(C) 100

(D) 120

(E) It cannot be determined from the information given.

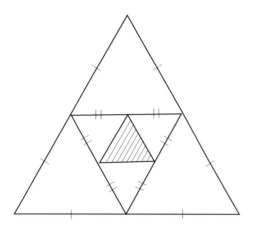

49.

In the figure above each triangle is equilateral, what fraction of the largest triangular region is shaded?

(A) $\dfrac{1}{16}$

(B) $\dfrac{1}{8}$

(C) $\dfrac{3}{16}$

(D) $\dfrac{1}{4}$

(E) $\dfrac{1}{2}$

50. How many integers k greater than 100 and less than 1000 are there such that if the hundreds and the units digits of k are reversed, the resulting integer is $k + 99$?

(A) 50

(B) 60

(C) 70

(D) 80

(E) 90

51. A call center responds to telephone inquiries between the hours of 9 am and 12 pm. Including the idle time, on average, it takes 1.5 minutes to answer an inquiry between 9 and 10 in the morning, 4.5 minutes between 10 and 11, and 5 minutes between 11 and 12. What is the fraction of total inquiries answered between 9 and 12 that the call center, on average, responds to between 9 and 10 in the morning?

(A) $\dfrac{30}{98}$

(B) $\dfrac{3}{22}$

(C) $\dfrac{30}{49}$

(D) $\dfrac{3}{9}$

(E) $\dfrac{9}{10}$

52. Which of the following is a solution of the equation $\dfrac{x^2+14x-240}{x+24} = 0$?

   (A) -24

   (B) -10

   (C) -8

   (D) 5

   (E) 10

53. A certain chemical reaction requires $\frac{4}{7}$ units of catalyst for every unit of chemical. How many students can perform an experiment if there are $20\frac{4}{7}$ units of catalyst available in the lab, and only one unit of the chemical is required for each student?

   (A) 33

   (B) 34

   (C) 36

   (D) 38

   (E) 40

54. Having collected data from a certain population, a statistician observes that the mean (arithmetic average) of the sample is 15. In order to increase the precision of his estimation procedure, the statistician shifts the data by subtracting 10 from every sample point and increasing variability by multiplying each observation by 1.5. What is the mean (arithmetic average) of the transformed sample?

   (A) 22.5

   (B) 20

   (C) 15

   (D) 7.5

   (E) 5

55. Three models ($A, B,$ and C) of cars are distributed among three showrooms. The number of cars in each showroom must be equal and each model must be represented by at least one car in every showroom. There are 19 cars of model A, 17 cars of model B, and 15 cars of model C. What is the maximum number of cars of model A in any showroom?

  (A) 17

  (B) 16

  (C) 15

  (D) 14

  (E) 13

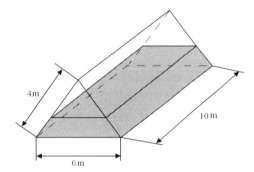

56.

A tank with an isosceles-triangular cross section with sides 4, 4, and 6 meters, has a length of 10 meters, and is currently resting on the 6 meter by 10 meter face. The tank is filled with water to the depth of 1 meter. If the tank is placed on a triangular face, what would be the depth of the water in the tank?

  (A) $\dfrac{5}{7}(\sqrt{7}-1)$

  (B) $\dfrac{10}{7}(\sqrt{7}-1)$

  (C) $\dfrac{10}{7}\sqrt{7}$

  (D) $\dfrac{10}{7}(2\sqrt{7}-1)$

  (E) $\dfrac{20}{7}(2\sqrt{7}-1)$

57. How many integers between 250 and 300, inclusive, can be evenly divided by NEITHER 3 NOR 5?

  (A) 33

  (B) 28

(C) 27

(D) 25

(E) 24

58. A store offers one item for 6 dollars or three items for 15 dollars. To purchase the set of three items is approximately what percent cheaper than the total cost of items purchased separately?

(A) 59%

(B) 58%

(C) 32%

(D) 19%

(E) 17%

59. Which of the following is the smallest?

(A) $\dfrac{3}{150}$

(B) $\dfrac{1}{20}$

(C) $\dfrac{13}{100}$

(D) $\dfrac{27}{50}$

(E) $\dfrac{9}{100}$

60. A car painting shop had a cubic painting chamber of 1000 cubic meters in volume. When a new and bigger car model was introduced, a parallelepiped section was added to a side of the painting chamber, which added fifty percent more volume to the original volume of the chamber. What are the dimensions in meters of the section added?

(A) $1:10:10$

(B) $2:10:10$

(C) $5:10:10$

(D) $20:10:10$

(E) $50:10:10$

61. Two secretaries, Sally and Lisa, type at even but difference paces. Sally is more experienced and types 80 characters per minute. Lisa, a beginner, can type only 30 characters per minute. On one day, Lisa starts typing before Sally. At some point, both have typed the same number of characters. Then both continue typing and Sally types 800 more characters until her computer breaks down. Assuming Lisa does not take any break, how long, in hours, will it take her to finish typing the same number of characters?

(A) $\dfrac{53}{180}$

(B) $\dfrac{4}{9}$

(C) $\dfrac{13}{18}$

(D) $\dfrac{15}{23}$

(E) $\dfrac{5}{18}$

62. Mary, Jane, and Lucy are typing a manuscript and are capable of completing the whole manuscript in $2\frac{1}{2}$ hours if they work together. If Mary alone can type the same manuscript in 10 hours, and Jane is capable of typing the complete manuscript in 6 hours, in how many hours can Lucy type the whole manuscript?

(A) $1\frac{1}{5}$

(B) $2\frac{1}{7}$

(C) 3

(D) 5

(E) $7\frac{1}{2}$

63. The cost of 150 erasers and 300 pencils is $75. At the same rate, what is the cost of 50 erasers and 100 pencils?

(A) $22.50

(B) $25.00

(C) $30.00

(D) $37.50

(E) $40.00

64. The cost of operating an aircraft consists of landing and take-off costs of l thousand dollars per one landing and take-off and fuel costs of f dollars per mile flown. How much, in thousands of dollars, does it cost per week to operate an aircraft which makes one landing and take-off per day and flies m miles per week?

(A) $7l + 1000fm$

(B) $\dfrac{7000l + fm}{1000}$

(C) $l + fm$

(D) $\dfrac{7l + 1000fm}{1000}$

(E) $7000lfm$

65. Of $3,500$ items manufactured by a machine, 80 percent pass the initial quality control, and the rest require additional testing. How many more items pass initial quality control than those which require additional testing?

(A) 110

(B) 400

(C) 700

(D) 2,100

(E) 2,800

66. If $a + b = 24$ and $a = 3b$, then $\sqrt{a} + \frac{a}{b} =$

(A) $3\sqrt{2}$

(B) $3\sqrt{3}$

(C) $3\left(\sqrt{2} + 1\right)$

(D) $3\left(\sqrt{2} + 2\right)$

(E) $4\left(\sqrt{2} + 1\right)$

67. To make a certain type of ale, a brewery must mix enzymes, flax, and barley in the proportion $3 : 5 : 7$ by volume. What is the largest amount in cubic meters of this mixture the brewery can obtain with one cubic meter of enzymes?

(A) $\dfrac{4}{5}$

(B) $\dfrac{5}{3}$

(C) $\dfrac{7}{3}$

(D)   4

(E)   5

68. Three types of aircraft fly three different routes which lengths are related as $1:3:5$. The ratio of the amount of fuel burnt over these routes in the same respective order is $5:3:1$. What are the ratios of their respective fuel consumption in units of distance per one unit of fuel burnt?

(A) $1:1:1$

(B) $1:3:5$

(C) $1:5:25$

(D) $5:3:1$

(E) $3:4:3$

69. During a volcanic eruption the particles of dust precipitate at the rate of $2\frac{1}{4}$ inches every three hours. If a volcano erupted for the first time for 2 hours and erupted again on the next day from 11:00 to 20:00, what was the total fall-out of particles in inches?

(A) $6\dfrac{3}{4}$

(B) $8\dfrac{1}{4}$

(C) $11\dfrac{1}{4}$

(D) $21\dfrac{3}{4}$

(E) $24\dfrac{3}{4}$

70. On the first day of the climb, mountaineers covered $\frac{5}{7}$ of the distance to the top, on the second day of the climb, they covered $\frac{1}{5}$ of the remaining distance. What fraction of the total climb do the mountaineers have to cover to reach the top on the third day?

(A) $\dfrac{1}{35}$

(B) $\dfrac{2}{35}$

(C) $\dfrac{8}{35}$

(D) $\dfrac{2}{7}$

(E) $\dfrac{4}{7}$

71. A repair shop can repair 3 fewer bicycles of Model 1 than three times the number of bicycles of Model 2. If one bicycle of Model 1 is replaced by two bicycles of Model 2, then the number of bicycles of each model repaired during the day is the same. What is the total number of bicycles that the shop can repair?

(A) 14

(B) 12

(C) 10

(D) 9

(E) 7

72. A certain MBA class had twice as many men as women. In a fund-raising event for a local school, each member of the class bought 10 raffle tickets at $5 per ticket. If the raffle ticket sales for the class totaled $3150, how many men were there in the class?

(A) 21

(B) 42

(C) 60

(D) 105

(E) 210

73. A particle starts to jump up and down consecutively from the origin for a fixed distance of L in each direction. It jumps for 100 seconds continuously each time for three times at three different constant speeds. Student 1 records all of the particle's returns to the origin when each of its jumps takes 2 seconds in either direction. Student 2 records only if each of the particle's jumps takes 3 seconds in either direction. Student 3 records only if each of the particle's jumps takes 5 seconds in either direction. Each of the students fills in his line in the table below. If each student is asked not to record beyond 100 seconds, what is the total number of entries that all three students record?

Student 1	*possible return times*
Student 2	*possible return times*
Student 3	*possible return times*

(A) None

(B) 25

(C) 50

(D) 51

(E) An infinite number of integers

74. From 1997 to 2003, the number of the U.S. produced motion pictures which did not use computer generated special effects decreased from 1,750 to 1,050. What was the percent decrease in the number of the U.S. produced motion pictures which are not using computer generated special effects over this period?

(A) 180%

(B) 80%

(C) 55%

(D) 46%

(E) 40%

75. The sum, s, of consecutive integers from 1 to n is given by the formula $s = \frac{n(n+1)}{2}$. What is the value of the sum if it is three times as large as the number of integers summed?

(A) 10

(B) 12

(C) 13

(D) 14

(E) 15

76. To reduce its stock of disposable contact lenses, a pharmacy sells 7 boxes for the price of 4. Given that a customer buys 7 boxes, approximately, what is the amount that she saves as a percent of what she would have spent?

(A) 22%

(B) 25%

(C) 42.9%

(D) 57.1%

(E) 75%

77. If $(625)(7)^2 = x(5^3)$, then $x =$?

    (A) 6125

    (B) 625

    (C) 343

    (D) 245

    (E) 125

78. A rectangle with dimensions 48 inches by 84 inches is to be divided into squares of equal size. Which of the following could be the length of the side of a square?

    (A) 8 inches

    (B) 12 inches

    (C) 15 inches

    (D) 16 inches

    (E) 20 inches

79. Let ▲ be an operation on variables x and y defined by the formula $x \blacktriangle y = 5 \left(\frac{xy}{y-x} \right)$ for every number x and y such that $x \neq y$. For which of the following pairs (x, y) does the value of $x \blacktriangle y$ equal 15?

    (A) $(1, 3)$

    (B) $(3, 0)$

    (C) $(2, 6)$

    (D) $(6, 2)$

    (E) $(4, -1)$

80. When going out, a party 'reveler' usually averages 40 dollars per hour for the first 3 hours of the night and 90 dollars per hour for each additional hour. How many hours does a party reveler usually spend if his average spending over night is 75 dollars per hour?

    (A) 5

(B) 7

(C) 8

(D) 10

(E) 12

81. As the side of a square was increased by 7 meters, the area of a square increased
     by 91 square meters. What was, in meters, the length of the side of this square
     before the increase?

     (A) 3

     (B) 6

     (C) 7

     (D) 13

     (E) 20

82. A substance is shipped in the concentrated form of 75 percent substance per
     gallon of water. To be usable the solution has to be diluted with water to achieve
     15-percent concentration. How many gallons of water does one need to add to the
     gallon of solution to obtain the useful concentration?

     (A) 4.00

     (B) 4.67

     (C) 5.00

     (D) 5.50

     (E) 7.00

83. Four consecutive even numbers are chosen between 4 and 20, inclusively. Suppose
     that w is the product of the numbers drawn, which of the following must be true?

     I. w is an integer multiple of 3.

     II. w is an integer multiple of 5.

     III. w is an integer multiple of 7.

     (A) I only

     (B) II only

     (C) I and II only

     (D) II and III only

     (E) I, II, and III

84. $\dfrac{\dfrac{1}{4}}{\left(\dfrac{4}{11}\right)\left(\dfrac{\frac{4}{5}}{\frac{3}{4}}\right)} =$

(A) $\dfrac{165}{256}$

(B) $\dfrac{16}{5}$

(C) $\dfrac{16}{15}$

(D) $\dfrac{1}{15}$

(E) $\dfrac{1}{33}$

85. GDP for Country U during year N:

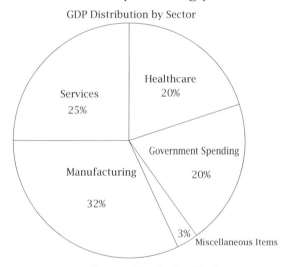

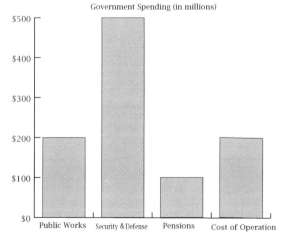

During Year N, the government's cost of operation was what percent of the total GDP of Country U?

(A) 4%

(B) 5%

(C) 8%

(D) 20%

(E) 25%

86. Making use of the information in the previous problem, if management consulting services in the economy of Country N have the same dollar value as miscellaneous items, what percent of total services is accounted for by management consulting services?

(A) 60%

(B) 15%

(C) 12%

(D) 6%

(E) 3%

87. At the beginning of a year, a certain computer problem requires 3.6×10^{11} calculations to solve, and a computer used to solve it is capable of $1,000,000$ calculations per second. At the end of the year, a new algorithm comes out which reduces the number of calculations by the factor of 10, and a new computer is built capable of performing twice as many calculations per second. What percent decrease in computing time (in hours) has been achieved?

(A) 60%

(B) 75%

(C) 85%

(D) 90%

(E) 95%

88. According to the national census conducted in the year 2000, deaths in Russia exceeded births by 0.3 million. The census showed that 1.2 million Russians died in the year 2000. Approximately, what percent of the population was born in Russia in the year 2000 if the same census counted that the total population was 167.8 million people?

(A) 0.0005%

(B) 0.005%

(C) 0.05%

(D) 0.5%

(E) 0.8%

89. A tanker departing from the Siberian port of Nakhodka is filled at 80 percent of capacity with heavy Siberian blend of oil, which is oil and sulphur solution with 30 percent sulphur content. 30 percent of the tanker's capacity is off-loaded in Murmansk to be reprocessed into heating oil for local customers. Then, the tanker proceeds to a North Sea terminal where it is loaded to capacity with the Brent blend of oil, in which sulphur content is negligible. Approximately, what percent of the resulting oil solution in the tanker is sulphur?

(A) 15%

(B) $18\frac{3}{4}$%

(C) 21%

(D) 24%

(E) 30%

Week	Number of data requests
1	20,000
2	20,000
3	15,000
4	5,000

90.

The table above shows the approximate number of data requests at the internet site of a new reality show for the first 4 weeks after it was the first time on the air. The cost of advertisement per week on the show's website was computed to be 10% of the product of the number of connections per week and the average length of a data request per week. But, the cost of advertisement may never fall below the cost of keeping the website operational, which is $2,000 per week. What was the total advertising revenue from the website, if the average length of a data request was estimated to be approximately 4 minutes?

(A) $8,000

(B) $18,000

(C) $20,000

(D) $24,000

(E) $25,000

91. A repair worker accidentally drops a hammer off the roof of the business school building at Columbia University. He notices that it takes 5 seconds for the hammer to reach the ground. A professor at Columbia University School of Business sees the hammer flying past her office window and notices that it reaches the ground in 3 seconds. How high is the professor's office above the ground if the distance S in feet covered by the dropped hammer is given by the formula $S = \frac{1}{2}gt^2$, where t is the time in seconds from the start of the drop by the worker and g is 32.2.

(A) 64.4

(B) 96.6

(C) 241.5

(D) 338.1

(E) 402.5

92. Of 440 new graduate students, 80 percent enrolled straight out of college and 20 percent transferred from a different graduate program. What is the difference between the number of new students who enrolled straight out of college and the new students with a previous graduate school experience?

(A) 44

(B) 220

(C) 240

(D) 264

(E) 352

93. Each night after 11pm the West Side Market disposes of its inventory of bagels by offering 5 bagels for one dollar. Bagel struck residents of the Upper West Side flood the market every night after that time, so the market has to regulate the flow of bagel mongers by increasing the price to 4 bagels for one dollar. The new price for each bagel is what percent greater than the old price?

(A) 0.25%

(B) 1%

(C) 5%

(D) 20%

(E) 25%

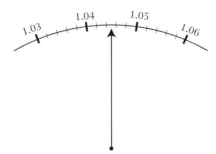

94.

An ammeter is calibrated to show the strength of electrical current. What is the strength of the electrical current shown?

(A) 1.030

(B) 1.039

(C) 1.040

(D) 1.045

(E) 1.048

95. After division by 3, all of the following have the same number of distinct prime factors EXCEPT

(A) 60

(B) 63

(C) 72

(D) 90

(E) 135

96. If $400,000 = 4^{n+1} \cdot 25^n$, then $n =$

(A) 1.5

(B) 2

(C) 2.5

(D) 3

(E) 3.5

97. A quarter of a page advertisement on the front page of the first section in a certain newspaper costs 10 thousand dollars, the same area advertisement on any subsequent page of the 10-page first section costs 2 thousand dollars. What is the total revenue in thousands of dollars from the first section if $\frac{1}{4}$ of every page of the first section is covered with an advertisement?

    (A) 15

    (B) 24

    (C) 28

    (D) 32

    (E) 34

98. A bus traveling along a mountain road covered d kilometers in the first 72 hours. The remaining 500 kilometers of the route the bus completed in h hours. What was the average speed in kilometers per day of the bus for the entire route?

    (A) $\dfrac{24(d + 500)}{72 + h}$

    (B) $\dfrac{dh + 72(500)}{72h}$

    (C) $\dfrac{d + 500}{24(72 + h)}$

    (D) $\dfrac{d}{3} + \dfrac{24(500)}{h}$

    (E) $\dfrac{d}{3} + 2\dfrac{1}{12}h$

99. The lateral surface area, A, of a regular tetrahedron is related to the length of its edge a by the following formula $A = \sqrt{3}a^2$. What is the difference in the length of the edge of the tetrahedron with the area of $625\sqrt{3}$ and the length of the edge of the tetrahedron with the area $196\sqrt{3}$?

    (A) 3

    (B) 9

    (C) 11

    (D) 90

    (E) 150

100. A McKenzie consultant hired by a chain of Japanese restaurants located in the Tyumen region of Russia wants to optimize raw fish deliveries. In order to do that, a consultant wants to know the fraction of customers who order sashimi. He estimates that 60 percent of customers order a raw fish dish, and of those customers 25 percent order sashimi. What is the fraction of the chain's customers who order sashimi?

    (A) 6%

    (B) 8%

    (C) 15%

    (D) 24%

    (E) 55%

101. A Ph.D. candidacy exam consists of 6 problems, each of which is worth 10 points. Among the 6 students who took the exam, each obtained a distinct score, the highest of which equaled the maximum score of 60 points. What could have been the least possible score obtained in the exam if the average (arithmetic mean) of the scores was 50 and all scores given were integers?

    (A) 1

    (B) 5

    (C) 10

    (D) 11

    (E) 20

102. If $1 = \frac{5}{4}k$, then $\frac{1}{k+5} =$

    (A) $\dfrac{5}{29}$

    (B) $\dfrac{4}{5}$

    (C) $\dfrac{6}{7}$

    (D) $\dfrac{7}{8}$

    (E) $\dfrac{29}{5}$

103. At a certain university, of all first year students, 160 students enrolled in an English Composition course, 200 students enrolled in an English Literature course, and 120 enrolled in both courses. If every first year student must enroll in at least one of these courses, how many first year students does this university have?

   (A) 480

   (B) 360

   (C) 320

   (D) 280

   (E) 240

104. $(226)^2 - (225)^2 =$

   (A) 1

   (B) 2

   (C) 5

   (D) 445

   (E) 451

105. During t_1 hours in the morning, customers arrive at a bank at the rate of r_1, and during t_2 hours in the afternoon, customers arrive at a bank at the rate of r_2. What is the average rate of arrival in customers per hour to the bank during the whole day?

   (A) $\dfrac{r_1 + r_2}{\frac{r_1}{t_1} + \frac{r_2}{t_2}}$

   (B) $\dfrac{r_1 + r_2}{t_1 + t_2}$

   (C) $\dfrac{r_1 t_1 + r_2 t_2}{t_1 + t_2}$

   (D) $\dfrac{t_1 + t_2}{r_1 t_1 + r_2 t_2}$

   (E) It cannot be determined from the information given.

106. A certain shoe store pays special attention to stocking shoes of sizes $8, 9, 9.5$, and 10. It stores $\frac{1}{3}$ as many shoes of size 10 as those of size 8, and $\frac{1}{2}$ as many shoes of size 8 as those of size 9. If the shoe store stocks equal numbers of shoes of size 9 and 9.5, what percent of shoes in the store accounts for shoes of size 8?

   (A) 10%

(B) 12.5%

(C) 15.25%

(D) 18.75%

(E) 20%

107. If $ad = bc$ for all positive a, b, c and d, which of the following is NOT always true?

(A) $\dfrac{a}{b} = \dfrac{c}{d}$

(B) $\dfrac{b}{a} = \dfrac{d}{c}$

(C) $\dfrac{b}{c} = \dfrac{d}{a}$

(D) $ad + \dfrac{a+b}{b} = bc + \dfrac{c+d}{d}$

(E) $\dfrac{a+b}{a} = \dfrac{c+d}{c}$

108. If $u \neq 5$ and $\frac{u^2-25}{4v} = \frac{u-5}{8}$, then, in terms of v, $u =$

(A) $\dfrac{v-10}{2}$

(B) $\dfrac{v-5}{2}$

(C) $v - 5$

(D) $v - 10$

(E) $\dfrac{v+10}{2}$

109. If a pair of numbers (a, b) is assigned the values $(-2, 2)$, which of the following equations does (a, b) satisfy?

I. $2a^3 - b^2 = -20$

II. $2a^2 - b^3 = 0$

III. $a^2 - 2b^3 = -4$

(A) I only

(B) I and II only

(C) I and III only

(D) II and III only

(E) I, II, and III

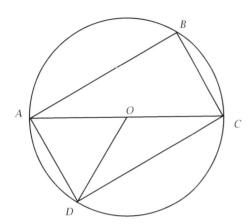

110.

The rectangle inscribed in the circle in the figure drawn above has a center at point O and a radius of length 6. The area of $\triangle ABC$ is $18\sqrt{3}$. What is the area of $\triangle ODC$ if points B, D, and O lie on the same line?

(A) 12

(B) $9\sqrt{3}$

(C) $6\sqrt{3}$

(D) 10

(E) $6\sqrt{2}$

111. What is 13.5 percent of $\frac{2}{27}$?

(A) 0.005

(B) 0.01

(C) 0.015

(D) 0.02

(E) 0.03

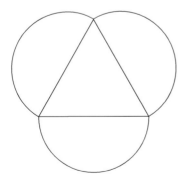

112.

Above is the base of a solid which is 5 centimeters in height. The base consists of an equilateral triangle and three semi-circles on each side of the triangle. Each side of the triangle is 40 centimeters. What is the volume in cubic centimeters of the solid?

(A) $2,400\pi + 400\sqrt{3}$

(B) $3,000\pi + 2,000\sqrt{3}$

(C) $12,000\pi + 2,000\sqrt{3}$

(D) $14,400\pi$

(E) $60,000\pi$

113. A product moves through a supply chain from a producer to a warehouse to a local retailer. A local retailer and a warehouse represent the same company, and the warehouse sells to the retailer at the same price that it obtains from its producer. The retailer's profit margin is 20 percent of the selling price, and the producer's profit margin is 20 percent of the cost. What percent of the cost is the sum of the profits collected by the producer and retailer?

(A) 20%

(B) 40%

(C) 50%

(D) 60%

(E) 75%

114. There are 360 single degree medical students and dual degree medical and doctoral students in an incoming class to a certain medical school. How many single degree students are in the class if the ratio of dual degree students to single degree students is 7 to 11?

(A) 20

(B) 80

(C) 140

(D) 220

(E) 280

115. Yachts in a fleet carry sails of two different colors, blue and orange, and of two different stripes, horizontal and vertical. 42% of yachts have sails with vertical stripes, and 70% of yachts carry blue sails. If 30% of the yachts which carry blue sails have vertical stripes on them, what is the ratio of yachts which have blue sails

with horizontal stripes on them to yachts which have orange sails with horizontal stripes?

(A) $\dfrac{7}{50}$

(B) $\dfrac{3}{21}$

(C) $\dfrac{49}{9}$

(D) $\dfrac{21}{29}$

(E) $\dfrac{35}{21}$

116. A computer programmer generates integers whose units digit is either 2 or 7. Which of the following when used as divisor for integers generated by the program can NOT produce an integer as a result of division?

(A) 17

(B) 11

(C) 10

(D) 6

(E) 3

117. If u and v are integers and $uv = -7$, then $(u + v)^3 =$

(A) -216

(B) 130

(C) 216

(D) 260

(E) It cannot be determined from the information given.

118. A three-digit number yields a remainder of 1 when it is divided by both 100 and 60. How many three-digit numbers are there with this property?

(A) None

(B) One

(C) Two

(D) Three

(E) Four

119. The price for a pair of socks is $5. The price for a 4-pair package of socks is $15. The 4-pair package is what percent cheaper per pair than 4 pairs purchased separately?

   (A) 80%

   (B) 75%

   (C) 55%

   (D) 25%

   (E) 20%

120. Manhattan Review hires a graduate student to update its database of 250 quantitative questions. If one student updates $1\frac{12}{13}$ percent of all problems per week, approximately, how many students, on average, does Manhattan Review have to hire to update its database of problems completely every quarter?

   (A) 2

   (B) 11

   (C) 4

   (D) 3

   (E) 10

121. If $99,999 = 90,909 + (9.09 \times m)$ then $m =$

   (A) $1,000$

   (B) 100

   (C) 10

   (D) $\dfrac{1}{100}$

   (E) $\dfrac{1}{1,000}$

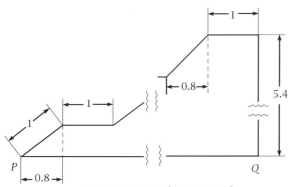

122.   Note: Figure not drawn to scale

A dam has a cross-section as in the figure above. All angles are right angles unless shown otherwise. The height of the dam is 5.4 meters. Each inclined section has a base of 0.8 meters wide and a slope of 1 meter wide. Each horizontal section is 1 meter wide. Assuming the entire cross-section of the dam consists of continuous inclined and horizontal sections, what is the total width of the dam from point P to point Q?

(A) 3.20

(B) 7.40

(C) 10.8

(D) 14.6

(E) 16.2

123. An investment asset pays to the owner $5\frac{3}{4}$ percent on the annual basis. If the same asset pays an annual interest rate of $5\frac{1}{4}$ instead of $5\frac{3}{4}$ on a semi-annual basis without compounding, what is the difference in each payment to the owner who holds $16,800$ dollars worth of this asset?

(A) $4.20

(B) $42.00

(C) $84.00

(D) $420.00

(E) $840.00

124. Economy, business, and the first class air fares on the same flight have an average price of $3,000. The business class fare costs $2\frac{1}{4}$ times as much as the economy class fare, and the first class fare costs $3\frac{1}{2}$ times as much as the economy class fare. What is the price of the business class ticket on this flight?

(A) $428

(B) $667

(C) $1,333

(D) $3,000

(E) $3,500

125. If u is an even integer, which of the following must be an odd integer?

    (A) $u + 12$

    (B) $u + 64$

    (C) $6u - 2$

    (D) $5u$

    (E) $7u + 1$

126. Initially, the price of an item had been expressed in terms of whole dollars. A store raised the price of an item by exactly 10 percent. Which of the following could NOT be the resulting price of the item?

    (A) $5.50

    (B) $7.60

    (C) $11.00

    (D) $12.10

    (E) $75.90

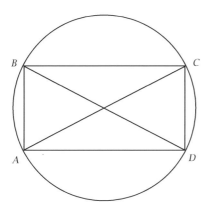

127.

Rectangle $ABCD$ with a perimeter of 60 is inscribed in a circle with a radius of $7.5\sqrt{2}$. What is the area of $ABCD$? (Note: Figure not drawn to scale.)

    (A) 150

    (B) 225

    (C) 450

    (D) 750

    (E) 900

128. The normal speed of a train is v kilometers per hour, and it takes 24 hours to cover a certain distance. Because of track repair, the train was not moving for the first w hours of the trip. Given that the train maintains constant speed when it moves, what was its speed, in kilometers per hour, during the time when the train was moving, if the train completed the route in 24 hours with an average speed of v kilometers per hour?

    (A) $12v$

    (B) $24v$

    (C) $\dfrac{24v}{w}$

    (D) $\dfrac{24v}{24-w}$

    (E) $\dfrac{24v}{24vw-w}$

129. How many of the integers between 37 and 57 are even?

    (A) 21

    (B) 20

    (C) 11

    (D) 10

    (E) 9

130. The greatest common divisor of $5^3 \cdot 11^2 \cdot 13$ and $5^2 \cdot 7^2 \cdot 11$ is?

    (A) $5 \cdot 11$

    (B) $5^2 \cdot 11$

    (C) $5^3 \cdot 11^2$

    (D) $5 \cdot 7 \cdot 11 \cdot 13$

    (E) $5^3 \cdot 7^2 \cdot 11^2 \cdot 13$

131. Which of the following is equal to $\frac{7}{12}$ of 1.52?

    (A) $\dfrac{42}{5}$

    (B) $\dfrac{21}{25}$

    (C) $\dfrac{133}{150}$

(D) $\dfrac{91}{300}$

(E) $\dfrac{9}{25}$

132. A bicycle rider calibrated his distance measuring device at a shop at the entrance to the bridge. On the bridge, due to vibration of the bridge, the device malfunctioned and underestimated the distance by 10 centimeters for every 15 meters traveled. What was the distance in meters shown by the device at the end of the bridge, if the length of the bridge is known to be 1800 meters?

   (A) 1698

   (B) 1704

   (C) 1710

   (D) 1779

   (E) 1788

133. $u = \left(\dfrac{1}{9}\right)^2, v = \dfrac{1}{3}, w = \sqrt{\dfrac{1}{81}}$

   The values of $u, v,$ and w are shown above. Which of the following is correct?

   (A) $u < v < w$

   (B) $u < w < v$

   (C) $v < w < u$

   (D) $w < u < v$

   (E) $w < v < u$

134. A Wall Street firm hired 140 students with an MBA degree and 40 students with an MA degree. The cost of hiring a student with an MA degree is half of that for the student with an MBA degree. What percent of the total cost of hiring is the cost of hiring all of the MA students?

   (A) 10%

   (B) 12.5%

   (C) 15%

   (D) 20%

   (E) 25%

135. A rectangular swimming pool has the perimeter of 200 meters and the constant depth of 3 meters. If the length of the pool is 20 meters greater than its width, how much water, in cubic meters, is required to fill the pool?

    (A) 2, 400

    (B) 4, 800

    (C) 7, 200

    (D) 9, 000

    (E) 24, 000

136. For all values of $u \neq 3$, $\dfrac{4u^2 - 20u + 24}{4u - 12} =$

    (A) $u + 3$

    (B) $u - 3$

    (C) $4u + 3$

    (D) $u - 2$

    (E) $4u + 12$

137. When Gary bought a boat, he found out that the municipality charged him 7 percent tax for marina services. If Gary paid $6, 885.45$ for the boat, what was the price of the boat before marina services tax?

    (A) 6, 012.34

    (B) 6, 335.00

    (C) 6, 435.00

    (D) 7, 111.05

    (E) 7, 367.43

138. A container used in large container ships has dimensions of $4 \times 6 \times 20$ meters. It is usually filled with smaller boxes which are 4 meters by 3 meters by 2 meters long. What is the maximum number of smaller boxes that can fit in a container?

    (A) 25

    (B) 20

    (C) 18

    (D) 12

    (E) 10

139. $\left[1 - \left(\dfrac{5}{6}\right)^2\right]^2 =$

    (A) $-\dfrac{1}{6}$

    (B) $\dfrac{1}{216}$

    (C) $\dfrac{1331}{4665611}$

    (D) $\dfrac{121}{1296}$

    (E) $\dfrac{11}{36}$

140. If u, v and w are non-zero numbers such that $0 < u < v \le 1$ and $w = \dfrac{v}{u}$, which of the following cannot be true?

    (A) $w \le 1$

    (B) $wu = 1$

    (C) $w = 2v$

    (D) $w > 0$

    (E) $u < w$

141. Three balls are drawn (without replacement) from an urn containing 5 blue balls, 4 green balls, and 3 yellow balls. What is the probability of drawing a blue ball, green ball, and yellow ball, in that order?

    (A) 1/220

    (B) 1/60

    (C) 5/144

    (D) 1/22

    (E) 47/60

142. One bag contains 3 white and 4 black balls; a second bag contains 2 white and 5 black balls. If one ball is drawn from each bag, what is the probability of drawing one black and one white ball?

    (A) 8/49

    (B) 15/49

    (C) 23/49

(D)   31/49

(E)   38/49

143.   Box I contains 4 red balls and 6 blue balls. Box II contains 3 red balls and 5 blue
       balls. A six-sided die is rolled. If the result is an odd prime number, a ball is
       chosen from Box I. If it is not, a ball is chosen from Box II. What is the probability
       of drawing a blue ball?

       (A)   31/80

       (B)   1/2

       (C)   49/80

       (D)   73/120

       (E)   37/60

144.   There are 6 people at a party sitting at a round table with 6 seats: A, B, C, D, E
       and F. A cannot sit next to D and F at the same time. How many ways can the 6
       people be seated?

       (A)   720

       (B)   120

       (C)   108

       (D)   84

       (E)   48

145.   5 blue marbles, 3 red marbles, and 4 purple marbles are placed in a bag. There are
       no other marbles in the bag. If 4 marbles are drawn without replacement, what is
       the probability that the result will not be 2 blue and 2 purple marbles?

       (A)   4/33

       (B) $(5/36)^2$

       (C)   1/2

       (D) $(31/36)^2$

       (E)   29/33

146. Three integers are chosen at random between 0 and 9, inclusive. What is the probability that each number is different?

    (A) 18/25

    (B) 4/5

    (C) 81/100

    (D) 9/10

    (E) 1

147. A committee is to be formed from 8 Republicans, 6 Democrats, and 4 Independents. The committee needs to be comprised of 4 Republicans, 3, Democrats, and 2 Independents. In how many ways can the committee be formed?

    (A) 4800

    (B) 8400

    (C) 9600

    (D) 13200

    (E) 14400

148. Four colors of cloth are available to be made into flags. How many vertically striped flags can be created if the flag can have up to four stripes and no color can be used more than once?

    (A) 24

    (B) 48

    (C) 60

    (D) 64

    (E) 256

149. A darts player's probability of hitting a bull's-eye is 3/5. What is the probability that he hits the bull's-eye for the first time on his third throw?

    (A) 8/125

    (B) 9/125

    (C) 12/125

    (D) 18/125

    (E) 27/125

150. Forty raffle tickets are sold to forty individuals, including one to each member of a family of three. Two prizes are to be raffled and one person cannot win both prizes. What is the probability that the family wins at least one prize?

    (A)   1/260

    (B)   3/40

    (C)   19/130

    (D)   12/13

    (E)   259/260

Chapter 2

Math Training Set – Data Sufficiency

Here are the five answer choices:

(1) Statement (1) alone is sufficient, but statement (2) alone is not sufficient

(2) Statement (2) alone is sufficient, but statement (1) alone is not sufficient

(3) Both statements TOGETHER are sufficient, but NEITHER statement ALONE is sufficient

(4) EACH statement ALONE is sufficient

(5) Statements (1) and (2) TOGETHER are NOT sufficient

1. What is the charge per hour of the 1st year associate at a law firm?

   (1) The 3rd year associate charges $300 per hour.

   (2) The 2nd year associate charges $1\frac{1}{2}$ times more than the 1st year associate, and the 3rd year associate charges two times more than the 2nd year.

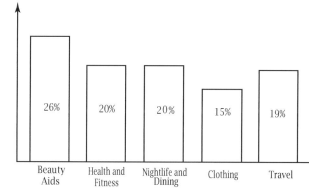

2.

During a certain year Michelle spent her annual trust fund allowance according to the chart above. How much did Michelle spend on clothing?

   (1) She spends $30,000 during the year on spas.

   (2) She spent $20,000 traveling.

3. Is $u > v$?

   (1) $0 < u < \frac{5}{6}$

   (2) $\frac{2}{3} < v < 1.0$

4. The capacity of the river tanker R is 50 percent greater than the capacity of the sea-going tanker S. How many more gallons of oil are currently in tanker R than in tanker S?

    (1) Tanker R is 90 percent full; tanker S is 40 percent full.

    (2) When full, tanker R contains $40,000$ gallons of oil.

5. Is q a negative number?

    (1) $-4q$ is a negative number.

    (2) $-q$ is a negative number.

6. Is 20 the average (arithmetic mean) of u, v, w, and 20?

    (1) $u + v + w = 60$

    (2) $u - v + w = 20, u + v - w = 16$

7. Car P and car Q competed in the same 300-kilometer race. What was the average speed of car P?

    (1) Car P completed the race in 3 hours and 40 minutes.

    (2) Car Q, at an average speed of 100 kilometers per hour, completed the race 40 minutes before car P crossed the finish line.

8. Is $p > q$?

    (1) $p^3 > q^3$

    (2) $p - q > 0$

9. At the time of admission, 35 percent of all doctorate students at a particular business school have a Ph.D. in a non-business related field. Meantime, 45 newly admitted students have a master's degree as their highest degree. Exactly how many Ph.D. students are there at this business school based on the following statistics at the time of admission for the entire program?Âă

    (1) 35 have a doctorate degree completed in a non-business related field.

    (2) 45 percent have a master's degree as their highest degree.

10. A triple of positive integers is defined to be a Pythagorean triple if and only if the sum of squares of the two of them equals the square of the third. If triangle S has sides whose lengths form a Pythagorean triple and triangle R has sides whose lengths are integers, do the side lengths of triangle R form a Pythagorean triple?

   (1) R has area which is a multiple of the area of S.

   (2) R and S are similar triangles.

11. The remainder of a positive integer w when it is divided by 2 is?

   (1) w is a multiple of an odd integer.

   (2) w is a multiple of 5.

12. If the ratio of job applicants with a doctorate degree to job applicants with an MBA degree for positions at Company G in 1999 was $\frac{1}{5}$, what was the ratio of applicants with a doctorate to applicants with an MBA for positions at company G in 2003?

   (1) Company G received 20,000 more MBA applicants in 2003 than in 1999.

   (2) Company G received 2,000 more Ph.D. applicants in 2003 than in 1999.

13. For each day at sea a sailor is paid a fixed sum. For each day ahead of the scheduled arrival time, he gets twice the regular daily earnings. If the total time at sea was scheduled for 20 days and a sailor earned a total of 3,850 dollars for the entire trip, how many days ahead of schedule did the ship arrive?Âă

   (1) If the ship had arrived one day ahead of the schedule, the sailor would have earned 4,200 dollars.

   (2) The sailor's regular daily earnings were $175.

14. Because of economies of scale, the cost of production of the second gadget is half the first one which costs c dollars to produce. The production of the third gadget costs half of the second, etc. What is the value of c?

   (1) The sum of the costs of the third and fourth gadgets is $9.

   (2) The sum of the costs of the second and the ninth gadget is $\frac{24(2^7+1)}{2^8}$ dollars.

15. If Q and R denote the nonzero digits of a three-digit number QRR, is QRR divisible by 3?

   (1) RR is divisible by 6.

   (2) RR is divisible by 2.

16. A direct flight from Lima to Cuzco was diverted to Arequipa due to unexpected bad weather. 163 passengers were on the flight when it finally arrived at Cuzco. How many passengers boarded the flight in Arequipa?Âă

   (1) When the plane took off from Lima, 184 people were on board.

   (2) 30 people chose to disembark at Arequipa and did not re-board the flight.

17. What is the area of $\triangle ABC$?

   (1) The measures of three angles are related as $1 : 2 : 3$.

   (2) The triangle's longest side is 10.

18. A retailer buys t-shirts from a wholesaler in lots of 25 t-shirts each. What is the wholesale price of a lot of t-shirts?

   (1) The retailer sells a single t-shirt for $4.80.

   (2) The retailer sells t-shirts at 20 percent above the wholesale price.

19. Are there exactly 4 distinct keys that are working on the old typewriter?

   (1) An old typewriter is defective in such a way that its blank key is not functioning, and the typewriter allows only 4 letters per word by forcing a space character to be inserted after each four-letter word. A monkey sitting at the typewriter is aware of this peculiarity and presses only distinct keys for each four-letter sequence. Some keys of this typewriter are not functioning.

   (2) A monkey is able to create only 24 distinct four-letter words.

20. If z is an integer, is $\frac{z}{3}$ an odd integer?

   (1) z is a multiple of 3.

   (2) z is a multiple of 9.

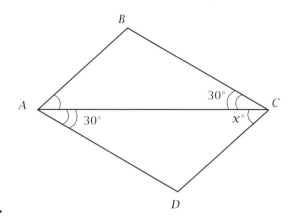

21.

∠*BAC* = ∠*ACD*, and the length of *AC* is 4. What is the area of the quadrilateral *ABCD* above?

   (1) *AB* = 2 and *BC* = $2\sqrt{3}$

   (2) *x*° = 60

22. *Q* is a set of integers and 11 is in *Q*. Let *q* denote any element in the *Q* set. Is every positive multiple of 11 in *Q*?

   (1) *q* + 11 is in *Q*.

   (2) *q* − 11 is in *Q*.

23. Does *q* have a distinct value?

   (1) $(2q - 3)^2 = q^2$

   (2) $\sqrt{12 - q} = 3$

24. If the product of *a* and *b* is strictly positive, is the sum of *a* and *b* greater than zero?

   (1) $b > a^4$

   (2) *b* = 5*a*

25. If 6*a* + *b* = 48, what is the value of *b*?

   (1) $4a^2 = 50$

   (2) 4*a* = *b* + 2

26. Some tickets to the men's and women's final of a certain tennis tournament are given away, the rest are sold at the box office. The ratio of the total number of tickets to the men's final to the total number of tickets to women's final is 3 to 2. Of the total number of tickets for both finals, what fraction was purchased at the box office?

    (1) The total number of men's final tickets and women's final tickets is 1240.

    (2) Of the men's final tickets, exactly 90 percent were purchased, and of the women's finals tickets, exactly 80 percent were purchased.

27. How much in royalties does a script writer get for a movie project, which costs $30 million to produce?

    (1) The producers pay to the script writer an initial fee of $25,000 when the script is received.

    (2) The script writer receives 3 percent of the box office gross receipts in excess of the cost of production.

28. A share of company P is 20 percent more expensive than a share of company Q. What is the ratio of the total value of shares outstanding of company Q to the total value of shares outstanding of company P?

    (1) The trading volume of shares of company Q is 25 percent more than that of company P.

    (2) The value of shares outstanding of company Q is $6,000,000 and the value of shares outstanding of company P is $8,000,000.

29. How much water is needed in the mixture used by a baker to prepare the dough for a wedding cake?

    (1) 50 guests are expected to be present at the wedding.

    (2) The amount of dough needed is 20 kilograms, and the dough is composed of water, flour, and yeast in the proportions $3:7:2$ by weight, respectively.

30. What is the value of u?

    (1) $\frac{7}{u} - 4 = 10$

    (2) $\frac{32}{16} = \frac{1}{u}$

31. If $u = v^4$, what is the value of $\frac{v}{u}$?

   (1) $u = 16$

   (2) $uv = 32$

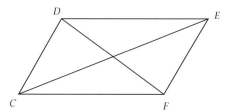

32.

   In the quadrilateral $CDEF$, $CD//EF$ and $DE//CF$. Do all sides of $CDEF$ have the same length?

   (1) $CE = DF$.

   (2) All angles of $\triangle CDF$ are the same.

33. What is the area of triangle R?

   (1) The base of triangle R is 15.

   (2) The ratio of the altitude dropped from the vertex opposite the base is related to the base of R is 5 to 1.

34. Is the integer y even?

   (1) $y - 7$ is odd.

   (2) $\dfrac{y}{\frac{1}{2}}$ is even.

35. If $x \neq 0$, is x equal to -1?

   (1) $x^5 = x$

   (2) $x^2 = -x$

36. A transmitter is located directly west of a receiver and directly north of a relay station built to circumvent a natural obstacle located directly between the transmitter and the receiver. If the obstacle were absent, given that the speed of the signal is known and constant, how much less time would it take for a signal to reach the receiver?

    (1)   The distance from the relay station to the receiver is 100 kilometers.

    (2)   The distance from the transmitter to the relay station is equal to 60 percent of the distance from the relay station to the receiver.

37. A pharmacy offers customers both a patented and a generic version of a certain drug. The pharmacy makes a profit of 20 percent of the cost on every box of the patented version, and it makes a profit of 5 percent of the cost on every box of the generic version. During a certain time period, which version of the drug yields a greater dollar profit to the pharmacy?

    (1)   The pharmacy pays more to the wholesaler per box for the patented version than for the generic version.

    (2)   The pharmacy sells 30 percent more of the generic version of the drug by weight than the patented version.

38. If $\triangle$ denotes an operation with two real numbers, what is the value of $x \triangle y$?

    (1) $x \triangle y = \frac{x^3}{y} + \frac{y^2}{x}$ for all x and y.

    (2) $x = 3$ and $y = 5$

39. How many seconds long is time period U if U can be no longer than a day?

    (1)   Time period U lasts from $13:59:00$ until $14:02:00$.

    (2)   Time period U lasts from $1:59:00$ pm until $2:02:00$ pm.

40. The surface area of a parallelepiped P is?

    (1)   The volume of P is 24 square meters.

    (2)   The height of P is 200 centimeters.

41. If u, v, and w are the lengths of the two sides and a diagonal of a parallelogram, respectively, is $w > 13$?

   (1) $u + v = 13$

   (2) $u = 10$

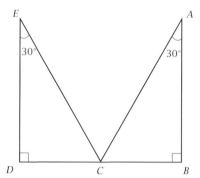

42.

While snail R starts to move from point A to C via AC directly, snail S starts to move from point B to C via BC directly. After the snails meet at point C, R moves to D with S's former speed, while S moves to E with R's former speed. Do the snails reach their destinations simultaneously?

   (1) S moves with the speed of 1 centimeter per minute.

   (2) R moves twice as fast as S.

43. In 1942, was the number of people drafted to the army of Country X greater than three times the number of people drafted to the army of Country Y?

   (1) In 1942, there were approximately 0.7 million more people drafted to the army of Country X then those drafted to the army of Country Y.

   (2) In 1942, the $300,000$ Adventist Christians made up 20 percent of the draft to the army of Country X, and the $141,000$ Evangelists made up 30 percent of the draft to the army of Country Y.

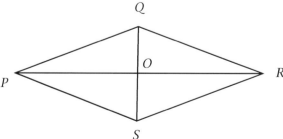

44.   A computer generates paths along the vertices of the parallelogram above. It moves in such a way that its path always consists of a side, a diagonal, and then a side and it never ends at the same vertex it begins with, i.e., $PQ \rightarrow QOS \rightarrow SR$. For each vertex on a path, the computer generates a random number. The sum of the numbers on one diagonal is equal to the sum on the other. For a given path, what is the number generated for vertex P?

   (1) The sum of Q and R is always 15 and S carries number 4.

   (2) The intersection of the diagonals, O, carries number 2.

45. A fraternity wants to enroll members of the college rowing team as members. The result of the fraternity's effort to recruit new members from the rowing team exceeds the fraternity's expectation by 20 percent. Assuming that the rowing team admits only males, what is the total number of people on the rowing team?

   (1) The goal was to enroll 15 percent of the members of the rowing team.

   (2) The number of rowing team members enrolling as new fraternity members was 40.

46. How many prime numbers are there strictly greater than 5 and less than the integer k?

   (1) $20 < k < 34$

   (2) $17 < k < 33$

47. What is the value $a^3 - b^3$?

   (1) $a^2 + ab + b^2 = 0$

   (2) $a - b = 3b$

48. Is $uv > 0$?

   (1) $u^2 v^3 < 0$

   (2) $uv^2 < 0$

49. If Z is an infinite subset of real numbers, is there a number in Z that is greater than every other number in Z?

   (1) Every number in Z is divisible by 5.

   (2) Every number in Z is a negative multiple of a prime number.

50. Is $\frac{u}{v}$ equal to 15?

   (1) $\frac{u}{v} + 5 = 20$

   (2) $\frac{u}{v} - 5 = 10$

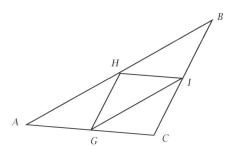

51.

In the figure above, $\triangle IGH$ is inscribed in $\triangle ABC$ in such a way that $HG\|BC$, $AB\|GI$, and $HI\|AC$. What is the length of AB times the length of HG?

   (1) $AB = 10$.

   (2) $BC \cdot GI = 24$

52. A set of Manhattan Review practice questions for all sections of the GMAT is l centimeters long, m centimeters wide, and n centimeters thick. These sets are shipped in a box which is l centimeters wide and m centimeters deep. How long does the box have to be to enable the shipping of 30 sets per box?

   (1) $n = 5$

   (2) $m = 20$ and $l = 27.5$

53. John, Pete, and Tim are running 100-meter races to prepare for a championship. Each of the runners won at least one of the heats. Which one of the three runners won the most races?

   (1) Tim won $\frac{3}{7}$ as many races as Pete.

   (2) Pete won $\frac{7}{3}$ as many races as John.

54. The average (arithmetic mean) of a professor's salary at University M is s. Is the average salary of a professor at University D at least 25 percent higher than that for a professor at University M?

  (1) At University M, the budget allocates $\$3,500,000$ for faculty remuneration.

  (2) At University D, the budget allocates $\$6,000,000$ for faculty's salaries.

55. A yacht club conducts a training race every Friday and Sunday during the summer months weather permitting. If the club was able to conduct a race every Friday and Sunday in the month of July, how many races were there that month?

  (1) There were five Tuesdays in the month.

  (2) The twenty-fifth of July was a Thursday.

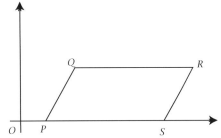

56.

Quadrilateral $PQRS$ has $PQ\|RS$ and $QR\|PS$. What is the area of $PQRS$?

  (1) The coordinates of point P are $(2,0)$, and the coordinates of point R are $(8,2)$.

  (2) The coordinates of point S are $(6,0)$.

57. Is ϵ equal to the average (arithmetic mean) of ζ, η, ψ, ξ and ν?

  (1) $\zeta + \eta + \psi + \xi + \nu = 5\epsilon$

  (2) $\dfrac{\zeta + \eta + \psi + \xi + \nu}{10} = \dfrac{\epsilon}{2}$

58. What is the value of τ?

  (1) $\tau(\tau - 1)^2 = 4\tau$

  (2) τ is an integer.

59. If $\triangle$ represents either ordinary division or ordinary multiplication, which does it represent?

    (1) $3 \triangle 1 = 3$

    (2) $0 \triangle 3 = 0$

60. The base of the roof of a building has a pentagonal shape. The roof is constructed as a regular pyramid with a pentagon as its base. What is the total area of the lateral segments of the roof?

    (1) The base of the pyramid has a perimeter of 30 meters.

    (2) The faces of the pyramid are equal triangles.

61. Let u, v, and w denote the lengths of three separate line segments. In order for u, v, and w to represent the lengths of three sides of a triangle, what value must v exceed?

    (1) $w = u + 5$

    (2) $u = 2$ and $w = 7$

62. What is the value of the two-digit number z?

    (1) The tens digit is twice the units digit.

    (2) The sum of two digits is 6.

63. How many students does the Gotham City School of Business enroll each year if?

    (1) The administration wants to maintain the faculty to students ratio of 2 to 15.

    (2) The administration also wants to maintain the size of each cluster of students to be 60 students.

64. If x and y are positive integers, is $x + y^2$ odd?

    (1) y is odd.

    (2) x is odd.

65. If r, s, and t are integers, is $rs + t$ divisible by 2?

    (1) r is divisible by 3, and s is even.

    (2) t is divisible by 3.

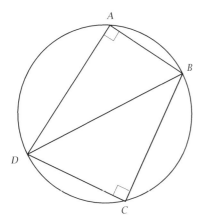

66.

    What is the area of region $ABCD$ shown above?

    (1) $AC = BD = 20$

    (2) $AB = DC$

67. What is the capacity of a fire reservoir, in thousands of cubic meters of water, which is currently filled up to three quarters of its capacity?

    (1) If 3×10^3 thousands of cubic meters of water were pumped into the reservoir, it would be filled to $\frac{7}{8}$ of its capacity.

    (2) If 6×10^3 thousand cubic meters of water were removed from the reservoir, if would be filled to $\frac{1}{2}$ of its capacity.

68. If u is a multiple of prime number v, is u a multiple of v^2?

    (1) $v < 6$

    (2) $u = 42$

69. How many thousands of gallons of water does a reservoir have?

    (1) If $\frac{1}{3}$ of the water in the reservoir were released, then the reservoir would be filled to $\frac{1}{2}$ of its capacity.

    (2) If 60 thousand gallons of water were pumped into the reservoir, it would be filled to capacity.

70. If $uv \neq 0$, what is the value of $\dfrac{u^4 v^3 - (uv)^3}{u^4 v^4}$?

    (1) $u = 3$

    (2) $v = 27$

71. Joern and Bin went on a year-long round-the-world backpacking tour starting January 1. Five days before the trip, each had opened a bank account. Then their insurance companies started to withdraw $300 from their accounts, respectively, on the first business day of each month. Assuming no other deposits or withdrawals, whose account had more money in it at the end of the year of travels?

    (1) On April 15 during the tour, Bin's account had twice as much money as Joern's account.

    (2) On June 15 during the tour, Bin's account had four times as much money as Joern's account.

72. Ice hockey teams R and U played against each other in the final games of numerous championships. Which of the teams won more than $\frac{1}{2}$ of these games?

    (1) The total number of games teams R and U played against each other in finals is 30.

    (2) Team R scored 128 goals in these matches, and Team U scored 203 goals in these matches.

73. A software company contracted its sister network technologies firm to upgrade its network and storage equipment. The sister firm charged the software company only for equipment and labor. What fraction of the total amount paid for the upgrade was the labor charge?

    (1) labor cost was $10,000$ less than the total cost of the upgrade.

    (2) Without the labor charge, the total cost of the upgrade would have been only $\frac{5}{6}$ as much.

74. An airplane was due north of a tropical island when hurricane warning arrived at noon. In what direction was the tropical island from the position of the airplane at 3 pm?

   (1) To circumvent the path of the hurricane, the airplane flew due west at 200 miles per hour from noon till 2 pm, and from 2 pm until 3 pm, it flew due south at 300 miles per hour.

   (2) At 3 pm, the airplane was exactly 450 miles from the tropical island.

75. Does $a = b$?

   (1) $\frac{a}{b} = \frac{b}{a}$

   (2) $(a - b)^2 = a^2 - b^2$

76. A father buys two toys for his son: a model of a plane and a model of a ship. What is the cost of a model of a ship?

   (1) The total cost of both toys was $40.

   (2) The ratio of the cost of the plane to the cost of the ship was $2 : 5$.

77. Is $p \cdot q \cdot r \cdot s$ equal to 16?

   (1) p, q, r, and s are each positive.

   (2) The sum of p, q, r, and s equals 2^3.

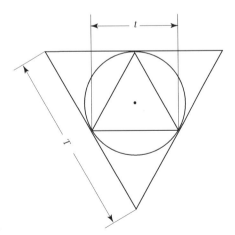

78.

   In the figure above, a circle is inscribed into an equilateral triangle with side T, and another equilateral triangle with side t is inscribed in the circle. What is the area of the large triangle?

    (1) $t = 12$

    (2) The radius of the circle is $4\sqrt{3}$.

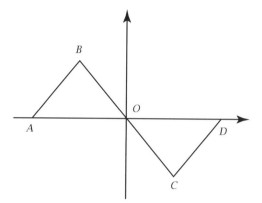

79.

In the figure above, the measures of angles $OAB, ODC,$ and DOC are equal. What is the area of $\triangle ABO$?

    (1) The coordinate of point C is $(6, -2\sqrt{5})$.

    (2) $AO = DO$.

80. What is the value of $\frac{91}{abc}$?

    (1) $3ab = 36$

    (2) $5abc = 65$

81. In the product $P_k = p_1 \cdot p_2 \cdot p_3 \cdot \ldots \cdot p_k$, if $p_1 > 0$ and $p_2 < 0$, is P_{12} negative?

    (1) All odd-numbered terms of the product have the same sign.

    (2) All even-numbered terms of the product have the same sign.

82. The total number of graduate students at a university is $6\frac{1}{4}$ percent higher this year than last year. How many graduate students does a university have this year?

    (1) Last year, 230 students completed their respective graduate programs at the university.

    (2) Last year, 1120 students were enrolled at the university's various graduate programs.

83. If all legal personnel at an intellectual property law firm are either patent evalua-tors or patent attorneys , what percent are patent evaluators?

    (1) Exactly 35 percent of the men and 30 percent of the women employed by this law firm are patent attorneys.

    (2) The ratio of the number of patent evaluators to the number of patent attor-neys is 7 to 13.

84. In a sequence of integer numbers in which each term is the square of the preceding term, what is the fourth term?

    (1) The last term is 6561.

    (2) The first term is 3.

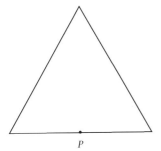

85.

Particle P moves counterclockwise along the edges of an equilateral triangle as above. What is the altitude of the triangle?

    (1) During one revolution about the triangle, the particle covers the distance of 6 meters.

    (2) P's speed is 1 meter per second.

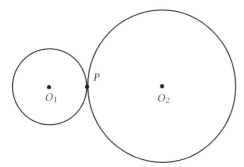

86.

Two flies move side by side around the circle centered at O_1 in the counter-clockwise direction. Later on, one of the flies starts moving around the circle centered at O_2 in the clockwise direction in such a way that it meets the other fly at point P when both complete one revolution about the centers O_1 and O_2, respectively. The speed of the fly revolving around O_2 is what percent of that revolving around O_1?

    (1)   The speed of the fly revolving around O_1 is 15 miles per hour.

    (2)   The radius of the smaller circle, O_1, is half the radius of the larger one, O_2.

87. In a clinical trial, patients reacted either according to pattern A or according to pattern B. What percent of the women participating in the trial exhibited the pattern A?

    (1)   There were $2,500$ women participating in the trial.

    (2) 859 trial participants exhibited pattern A.

88. A Cape Codder and a Screw Driver are solutions of vodka and cranberry juice, vodka and orange juices, respectively. What percent of Cape Driver, a solution of vodka, cranberry, and orange juices, would be vodka if Cape Driver were 4 parts Cape Codder and 5 parts Screw Driver? s

    (1)   Cape Codder is 20 percent vodka, and Screw Driver is 10 percent vodka.

    (2)   A glass fits 0.3 liters of Cape Driver.

89. Is rectangular block B a cube?

    (1)   At least two faces of rectangular block B are square.

    (2)   The volume of rectangular block B is 64.

90. Two heptathlon finalists, A and B, compete in seven events. The highest score for each event is 10 points. A competitor who wins 4 or more events wins the final. The competition continues until all competitors complete all seven events. Which of the competitors won the final?

    (1)   The total points of A is twice as many as those of B.

    (2)   Either A or B won the first four events in a row.

91. If u and v are positive real numbers, is $u > v$?

    (1) $\dfrac{u^3}{v} < 1$

    (2) $\dfrac{u^{\frac{1}{3}}}{v} < 1$

92. Mary purchased 28 books of literature, some of which were fiction. How many of the books did not contain fiction?

    (1) Of the books Mary purchased, the number containing fiction is equal to the number containing biographies.

    (2) Of the books Mary purchased, the number containing fiction is odd.

93. During a 3-year period, the Gross Domestic Product (GDP) of Country U changed by what percent from the first year to the second year?

    (1) The GDP of Country U enjoyed a constant growth rate both from the first to the second year and from the second to the third year in a certain 3-year period.

    (2) The GDP during the first year was 235 billion dollars. It increased to 338.4 billion dollars in the third year.

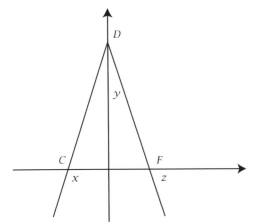

94.

    In $\triangle CDF$ above has $CD = DF$, what is the value of z?

    (1) $y = 30°$

    (2) $x = 120°$

95. Each of the 30 cars in the parking lot has a catalytic converter attached to either the engine only or the exhaust pipe only, or both the engine and the exhaust pipes. How many cars have just one converter attached to the engine only?

   (1) Of the 30 cars, 27 have a catalytic converter attached to the engine and 21 have a catalytic converter attached to the exhaust pipe.

   (2) Of the 30 cars, 3 have a catalytic converter attached to the exhaust pipe only.

96. A certain shipment of computer equipment contains two types of memory chips. One type has capacity of 128 megabytes (MB), the other has capacity of 256 MBs. What is the total capacity of all the chips in the shipment?

   (1) The total capacity of 128-MB chips is twice as much as that of 256-MB chips.

   (2) The shipment contains a total of 512 chips, and there are 8 times as many 128-MB chips as 256-MB chips in the shipment.

97. A liquor store sells Spanish and Italian red wine in bottles. Is the price of Spanish red wine per liter greater than the price of Italian red wine per liter?

   (1) The price for a bottle of Spanish red wine is 30 percent greater than the price for a bottle of Italian red wine.

   (2) A bottle of Spanish red wine contains 25 percent more wine than a bottle of Italian red wine.

98. A circle is contained in a square. What is the perimeter of the square?

   (1) The radius of the circle is 16 centimeters.

   (2) Each side of the square is tangent to the circle.

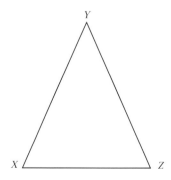

99.

$\triangle XYZ$ above is isosceles. What is its area?

(1) The perimeter of XYZ is 60.

(2) $XZ = 24$

100. On the night a certain university's team won, all of the 60 students living in a fraternity house were charged with driving in excess of a speeding limit or reckless driving, or both. How many member of this particular fraternity were charged with both speeding and reckless driving?

(1) Of the 60 students, 20 were charged with speeding only.

(2) Of the 60 students, 40 were charged with reckless driving and 32 were charged with speeding.

101. A rectangular parallelepiped's width, length, and height are related as $3 : 4 : 7$. What is the surface area of this solid?

(1) The width and length of the solid is 6 and 8.

(2) The volume of the solid is 672.

102. If z is a positive integer, does z have divisors different from 1 and z?

(1) $z < 5$.

(2) $3z < 13$.

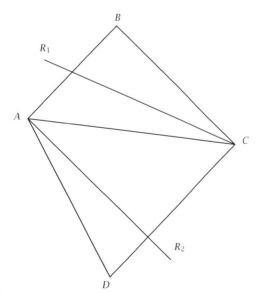

103.

R_1 bisects $\angle ACB$, and R_2 bisects $\angle CAD$. Is $R_1 \| R_2$?

(1) $AB = DC$.

(2) BD bisects AC.

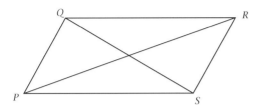

104.

The quadrilateral $PQRS$ above has $PQ \parallel RS$ and $PS \parallel QR$. What is the area of $PQRS$ if $QS = 8$?

(1) $\triangle QRS$ is equilateral.

(2) Segments QR and RS have equal length.

105. A ferry goes from a town on a peninsula to Island I_1 and to Island I_2. Which of the islands, I_1 or I_2, is closer to the town?

(1) It takes a ferry an average of 40 minutes to go from the town to I_1.

(2) It takes the same ferry an average of 40 minutes to go from I_1 to I_2.

106. A large rectangular pool with dimensions 75 meters by 100 meters is divided, using ropes, into 20 smaller rectangular sectors of equal dimensions. What are the dimensions of each rectangular section of the pool?

(1) One of the dimensions of each of the sectors is 15 meters.

(2) One of the dimensions of each of the sectors is 25 meters.

107. A hiking trip lasted for 12 days. For the first 10 days, what was the average (arithmetic mean) daily distance covered on foot?

(1) The total distance walked in 12 days was 300.50 miles, which included the distance of 20 miles per day for each day after the first 10 days.

(2) The average distance per day for the whole trip of 12 days was approximately 25 miles.

108. Is the positive integer z an even number?

    (1) If z is divided by 5, the remainder is 2.

    (2) If z is divided by 7, the remainder is 2.

109. The price of a kilogram of oranges is $0.25. What is the maximum amount of juice that can be squeezed out of oranges bought for $1.00?

    (1) The price of a bag of oranges is $2.80.

    (2) Every kilogram of oranges may yield from 200 to 300 milliliters of orange juice.

110. A shipping box contains between 60 and 70 items. How many items are there in the shipping box?

    (1) If the items in the box are counted in the sets of three, then there are two items remaining in the box.

    (2) If the items are counted in sets of 9, then there are two items remaining in the box.

111. Is u^3 equal to 64?

    (1) $u > 3$

    (2) $u < 5$

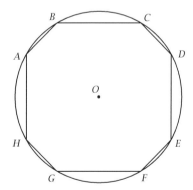

112.

In the figure above, the octagon $ABCD\ldots H$ is inscribed in the circle with the center at O. If the radius of the circle is 12, what is the area of the region inside the circle but outside of the octagon?

    (1) Rectangles $ABEF$ and $HGDC$ are equal, and $AB = AO$.

    (2) $AH < AB$

113. A certain grain contains only protein, carbohydrates, and fats. How many pounds of fats are contained in the 66 pounds of the grain?

   (1) By weight the grain is $\frac{5}{11}$ protein and $\frac{7}{22}$ carbohydrates.

   (2) By weight the grain contains 3 parts protein and 7 parts carbohydrates.

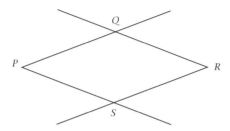

114.

   In the quadrilateral $PQRS$ above, is $PQ > RS$?

   (1) $PQ \| RS$

   (2) $PS \| RQ$

115. Is the statement $0 < u < 1$ true?

   (1) $0 < u^{\frac{1}{3}} < 1$

   (2) $u^4 = \dfrac{1}{16}$

116. The personnel department of the hospital H receives applications from doctors and nurses. How many nurses did hospital H hire last year?

   (1) Last year only $\frac{1}{5}$ of all job applicants were interviewed and only $\frac{1}{6}$ of those interviewed were hired.

   (2) Last year hospital H received applications from 300 nurses.

117. Two friends, Sasha and Masha, went out of town for a week-end. Sasha drove in one direction, and Masha drove back. If both friends each drove 240 miles, what was the average speed, in miles per hour, at which Sasha drove?

   (1) The average speed at which Masha drove was 60 miles per hour.

   (2) Sasha drove for exactly 4 hours.

118. What is the greatest common factor of positive integers u and v?

   (1) The greatest common factor of $\frac{u}{4}$ and $\frac{v}{4}$ is 11.

   (2) $\frac{u}{2}$ and $\frac{v}{2}$ are even.

119. If $v > 0$, what fraction is v of u?

   (1) $u = 3v$

   (2) $u + v = 72$

120. What is the area of a regular octagon?

   (1) Each side is 8 meters long.

   (2) The distance from the center of an octagon to the midpoint of one of the sides is $4\sqrt{3}$ meters.

121. The area, A, of an equilateral triangle inscribed into a circle is $\frac{3\sqrt{3}}{4}r^2$, where r is the radius of the circle. If C is the length of the circumference of the circle, what is r?

   (1) $\frac{A}{C} = \frac{8\pi}{3\sqrt{3}}$

   (2) $A > C + 1$

122. Is y equal to 3?

   (1) y satisfies $y^2 - 5y + 6 = 0$.

   (2) y satisfies $y^2 - 7y + 12 = 0$.

123.

A belt connects two pulleys as above. One of them, centered at T, is shaped as an equilateral triangle, the other, centere d at H, is an equilateral hexagon. If the triangle makes 100 revolutions per minute, how many does the hexagon make?

   (1) The length of TH is 12 meters.

   (2) The ratio of the perimeter of the triangular pulley to the perimeter of the hexagonal pulley is 1 to 6.

124. Was Pete's average running speed for the first two hours of his 42-kilometer marathon 12 kilometers per hour?

    (1) He ran the entire 42 kilometers in 3 hours.

    (2) He ran the last 18 kilometers in 1 hour.

Chapter 3

Math Training Set Solutions – Problem Solving

1. It is given that 10.8 grams make 9 percent of the yield. So, the total yield is

$$
\frac{10.8}{\frac{9}{100}} = 108 \times \frac{10}{9}
$$
$$
= 12 \times 10
$$
$$
= 120,
$$

and the percentage required is

$$
\frac{13.5}{120} \times 100 = \frac{4.5 \times 3}{3 \times 40} \times 100
$$
$$
= \frac{45}{4}
$$
$$
= 11.25.
$$

Another way to solve the problem is to make x the unknown percentage.

$$
\frac{x}{9\%} = \frac{13.5}{10.8}
$$

$$
x = \frac{13.5 \times 9 \times 0.01}{10.8}
$$
$$
= \frac{13.5 \times 0.1}{12}
$$
$$
= \frac{135}{12}\%
$$
$$
= 11.25\%
$$

Therefore, the best answer is (C).

2. One must be careful since the question asks for the number of offenses a driver can make before his license is revoked, which implies that 100 offense points are still 'good enough' to drive. Since the maximum number of points for which driving is still allowed is one hundred, a driver can be caught only 10 times while getting 19 points for his $10th$, and the last, offense as the table below shows.

offense	Points	Cumulative
1	1	1
2	3	4
3	5	9
4	7	16
5	9	25
6	11	36
7	13	49
8	15	64
9	17	81
10	19	100

Another quick way of calculation is:

$$
\begin{aligned}
1 + 3 + 5 + 7 + 9 + 11 + 13 \;\; + \;\; 15 + 17 + 19 \\
= \;\; (1 + 19) \times 5 \\
= \;\; 100
\end{aligned}
$$

Therefore, the best answer is (C).

3. The key to this question is to know that, by definition, the percent change in price is the difference of old and new prices divided by the old price, or, mnemonically, it is 'new minus old divided by old'. So, given the numbers of the problem, the percent change is

$$
\frac{30 - 75}{75} \times 100 = \frac{-45}{75} \times 100 = -60
$$

percent. Therefore, the best answer is (B).

4. Note that numerators and denominators of all fractions are multiples of 6 and 7, respectively. With this in mind, we can write the value of u as

$$
\begin{aligned}
u &= \frac{6}{7} + \frac{3 \times 6}{3 \times 7} - \frac{2 \times 6}{2 \times 7} \\
&= \frac{6}{7} + \frac{6}{7} - \frac{6}{7} \\
&= \frac{6}{7}.
\end{aligned}
$$

So, we have that

$$
\left(\frac{6}{7} - 1 \right)^3 = \left(-\frac{1}{7} \right)^3 = -\frac{1}{343}.
$$

Therefore, the best answer is (A).

5. u is an integer such that $35 < u < 41$. $13 \times 35 = 455$, and $13 \times 40 = 520$. So, (A) is eliminated since $13 \times 41 = 533 > 520$. (D) and (E) can be eliminated since $u \not\leq 35$. (C) is not possible since there is no integer between 6 and 9, inclusively, which, when multiplied by 3, produces a 0 as a units digit. Therefore, the best answer is (B) since $40 \times 13 = 520$.

6. Let the current populations of Countries S and J be denoted as s and j, respectively. The first sentence of the problem states that $j - s = 10$, and the second sentence states that $j + 0.5 \times 5 = 2(s + 0.5 \times 5)$. Since $j = s + 10$, $s + 12.5 = 2(s + 2.5)$, and $s = 7.5$. So, in 3 years Country S will have the population of $7.5 + 1.5 = 9$ million people. Therefore, the best answer is (C).

7. The key is to translate the first sentence into the formula

$$uv = 20 \times \frac{u - v}{v}.$$

Substituting the value of $v = 4$ into the formula above, we obtain that

$$4u = 5(u - 4), \ u = 20.$$

Therefore, the best answer is (C).

8. If n_2 and n_1 are two difference values of n, then $n_2 - n_1 = 30$. Adding and subtracting 42 from the left-hand side of the equality above does not change the equality. So, we have

$$n_1 - n_2 + 42 - 42 = (n_1 - 42) - (n_2 - 42) = 30.$$

Then, multiplying both sides of the equality by $\frac{5}{11}$ yields the difference in the values of m corresponding to n_1 and n_2, which is $30 \cdot 5/11 = 150/11$. Therefore, the best answer is (D).

9. The key to this question is to decompose 80 into its prime factors and using these prime factors to construct the factors of 80 that greater than $\sqrt{80}$. Since $9^2 = 81$, $\sqrt{80} < 9$. Since a factor is necessarily an integer, we are looking for factors which are greater than 9. Prime number decomposition of 80 is $2^4 \cdot 5$. To determine a

complete set of factors, we need to do it systematically.

$$2, 2, 2, 2, 5$$
$$2 \times 2 = 4$$
$$2 \times 5 = 10$$
$$2 \times 2 \times 2 = 8$$
$$2 \times 2 \times 5 = 20$$
$$2 \times 2 \times 2 \times 2 = 16$$
$$2 \times 2 \times 2 \times 5 = 40$$
$$2 \times 2 \times 2 \times 2 \times 5 = 80$$

So, the factors of 80 greater than $\sqrt{80}$ are $10, 16, 20, 40$, and 80 - five in total. Therefore, the best answer is (D).

10. The partitioning is done three times, and each partitioning resulted in 4 times more rectangles than the previous partitioning. So, the area is $4 \cdot 4 \cdot 4x = 64x$. Therefore, the best answer is (D).

11. The product of 13 consecutive integers always contains an even integer, so the product is always even. Therefore, the best answer is (B).

12. Imagine three boxes each of which contains a digit of the required type. The first box has a choice of three digits, specifically, $3, 5$, and 7, only. 2 is a prime but not an even number. The second box has a choice of four digits: $2, 3, 5$, and 7. And the third box has a choice of five digits: $1, 3, 5, 7$, and 9. The total number of three-digits numerals is the product of the number of choices that each box contains, i.e. $3 \times 4 \times 5 = 60$. Therefore, the best answer is (B).

13. The key to this question is to write N as a fraction $\frac{N}{1}$ and cross-multiply. So, we obtain

$$
\begin{aligned}
N(1 - pq) &= N - Npq \\
&= S, \\
N - S &= Npq, \\
p &= \frac{N - S}{Nq}.
\end{aligned}
$$

Therefore, the best answer is (A).

14. To obtain the answer, one could proceed in two ways. The first method involves looking at the hundreds column first (instead of the units column as many may be inclined to do). Notice that the sum of the digits $9, 7$, and 6 is 22, which means that the tens column produces a carry-over of 1. This means that the tens column sums to $10 + \star$. Now, summing the digits in the units column we obtain 15, which gives a carry-over of 1 to the tens column. So, the sum in the tens column is of the form $1 + 6 + \star + \star$. With this in mind, let us denote the digit indicated by $\star$ with the letter x and set up an equation,

$$10 + x = 1 + 6 + x + x.$$

Easy algebra gives us that $x = 3$.

The second method amounts basically to guessing. To obtain the answer, one should notice that the sum of the units column is $15 = 5 + 7 + 3$, which produces a carry-over of 1 to the tens column. So, the total sum of integers in the tens column equals to $6 + 3 + 3 + 1 = 13$, which points to the same best answer (B).

15. This question is solved by elimination. (A) may or may not be true. For example, if $x = 5$ and $y = -0.1$, then $x^2 + y^3 > 0$. (B) is not true for the same value of x and y. (C) is not true if $y = -5$ and $x = 0.1$, and (E) is not true because an odd power of a negative number is negative, and division by the positive x does not change the sign of the fraction. So, (D) is true because an even power of a negative number is positive, and the sum of two positive numbers is always positive. Therefore, the best answer is (D).

16. The solution is obtained by testing the answers against the conditions specified in the problem. Suppose, the average time is 13.2. Then the total time to paint the fence is $13.2 \times 4 = 52.8$, which leaves only 25.8 ($52.8 - 13 - 14 = 25.8$) hours in total for Ruth and Beth to complete the task. So, each of them must do it in less than 13 hours, and this is impossible since the least time to paint a side is 13 hours. Therefore, the best answer is (A).

17. The area, A, of any triangle, is given by the formula

$$A = \frac{1}{2}bh,$$

where h is the length of an altitude corresponding to a side with the length b. Since $A = 35$, $bh = 70$. The figure supporting the question shows that $b = 5k$, $h =$

$3k$, so $bh = 15k^2$. Substituting $bh = 70$, we have that $15k^2 = 70$. Simplifying,

$$k^2 = \frac{70}{15} = \frac{60 + 10}{15} = 4\frac{10}{15} = 4\frac{2}{3} = \frac{14}{3}.$$

Now,

$$k = \sqrt{\frac{14}{3}} = \frac{1}{3}\sqrt{42}.$$

Therefore, the best answer is (D).

18. Let y be the fixed sum that each oligarch receives. Then, x enjoys the following simple representation

$$x = 11y + 10.$$

Note that y must be even. If it were odd, then x would be odd as well since a product of two odd number is an odd number and adding 10, an even number, would still keep x odd. Now, proceed by elimination noticing that $11y$ is an even number, and if an odd number is added to $11y + 10$, the result is odd - not divisible by 22, an even number. This leads us directly to 12. Therefore, the best answer is (D).

19. The key here is to recall that any integer can be decomposed into a product of primes. A necessary and sufficient condition for a product of numbers to be divisible by (or to be a multiple of) any integer is that the prime number decomposition of this product contains that integer. For example, $24 = 2^3 \times 3$. So, it is divisible by (or is a multiple of) $2, 4, 6,$ and 8. Let us start with I. Do all consecutive triples between 10 and 19 have a 3 in their prime number decomposition? To be a multiple of a 3, a triple (by a triple, henceforth, we mean a consecutive triple) must contain one of the following: $12, 15, 18$. It is easy to see that every triple contains one of above numbers. So, I is true. How about II? To be a multiple of 4, a triple must contain either two even numbers or one of the following: 12, or 16. $13 \times 14 \times 15$ has neither of the above. So, (B), (D), and (E) are not true. To choose between (A) and (C), we must check if III is true. A triple is a multiple of 6, if it contains an even number and a multiple of 3 such as 15 or one of the following: $12, 18$. It is a trivial, but not an easy under time pressure check, that every triple satisfies the above condition. So, III is true, and (C) is the answer.

It is also convenient to consider the table below.

$$
\begin{array}{ccc}
10 & 11 & 12 \\
11 & 12 & 13 \\
12 & 13 & 14 \\
13 & 14 & 15 \\
14 & 15 & 16 \\
15 & 16 & 17 \\
16 & 17 & 18 \\
17 & 18 & 19
\end{array}
$$

If each row above is a representation of the product w, then it is easy to see that each row contains a multiple of 3. It is also easy to find that the product $13 \times 14 \times 15$ is not divisible by 4. As for option III, the first 3 rows contain 12. The next 3 rows contain the multiple of both 2 and 3, and the last two rows contain 18. Therefore, the best answer is (C).

20. The answer may be obtained in a number of ways. The first one is by elimination. If (D) were the answer, then before the transfer South Korea would have had

$$
\frac{1}{4}(300 - 60) = 60
$$

aircraft. So, the ratio of South Korean to North Korean aircraft after the transfer would have been

$$
\frac{60 + 60}{\frac{3}{4} \times 240} = \frac{2 \times 60}{\frac{3}{4} \times 4 \times 60} = \frac{2}{3}
$$

instead of $\frac{3}{5}$ as given. If (B) or (C) were answers, the we would have had fractional number of South Korean aircraft before the transfer. A similar computation as in case of (D) shows that (A) is not the correct answer either.

The second solution is based on scaling. Suppose that initially South Korea had 1 aircraft and North Korea had 3. Then South Korea and North Korea had 3 and 5 aircraft, respectively. But the number of North Korean aircraft remains constant, so we can pick an easy number for this constant, say, 15. So, initially, the South had 5 aircraft to make the ratio $\frac{1}{3}$ hold, and 9 aircraft after the transfer. This makes 4 transferred aircraft to be $\frac{1}{6}$ of the total 24. In terms of real numbers, it means that 60 transferred aircraft is $\frac{1}{6}$ of the total. So, the total is $60 \times 6 = 360$.

The third method is general. Let S be the number of aircraft in the South, and N

in the North. Before the ratio of S to N was 1 to 3:

$$\frac{S}{N} = \frac{1}{3}, \; 3S = N.$$

After the transfer the ratio $S + 60$ to N became 3 to 5:

$$\frac{S + 60}{N} = \frac{3}{5}, \; 5S + 300 = 3N.$$

Solving this system of equations, we obtain $S = 75$, and the total number of aircraft after the transfer became

$$75 + 60 + 3 \times 75 = 360.$$

Therefore, the best answer is (E).

21. The distributor wants a profit of 20 percent which is equal to $\frac{15 \times 20}{100} = \frac{15}{5} = 3$ dollars. So, the distributor's price of this item is \$18. Now, if a 20 percent commission is applied to the price, which a buyer pays for the item, the distributor must receive \$18 per item to satisfy his margin requirements. In other words, if a on-line store retains $\frac{1}{5}$ of the buyer's price as commission, then 18 is $\frac{4}{5}$ of the buyer's price. So, if a buyer pays x dollars for the item, then

$$18 = \frac{4}{5}x, \; x = \frac{18 \times 5}{4} = \frac{90}{4} = 22\frac{1}{2}$$

dollars. Therefore, the best answer is (D).

22. The answer comes from an application of the Pythagorean theorem and the right choice of right triangles.

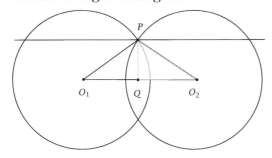

First, notice that $\triangle PO_1O_2$ is isosceles, and PQ is the altitude of $\triangle PO_1O_2$ by construction. Therefore, $\triangle PQO_2$ is a right triangle. In an isosceles triangle, an altitude dropped from the vertex where equal edges meet divides the base in two equal halves, O_1Q and QO_2. Each half is of length 8 since the halves make up O_1O_2. Now, the length of PQ is determined via an application of the Pythagorean theorem:

$$PQ = \sqrt{(PO_2)^2 - (QO_2)^2}$$
$$= \sqrt{10^2 - 8^2} = 6.$$

Therefore, the best answer is (C).

23. We need to compute the ratio of male applicants still competing for a spot after the fist round to the total number of applicants remaining after the first round. It is convenient to choose an arbitrary number of applicants, say, 80. So, out of 80, $\frac{3}{8} \times 80 = 30$ are male, of which only a third, i.e. 10, remain after the first round, and only $\frac{1}{4} \times 80 = 20$ of all the applicants, male and female, remain. So, the answer is $\frac{1}{2}$. Therefore, the best answer is (C).

24. The key is to use the fact that the sum of the angles in a triangle is $180°$. It follows that $x = 45°$, and $x + y = 60°$. So, $y = 15°$, and $2x - y = 90° - 15° = 75°$. Therefore, the best answer is (E).

25. The key to this problem is to remember that the sides of a $30° - 60° - 90°$ triangle are related as $1 : \sqrt{3} : 2$, and the sides of a $45° - 45° - 90°$ triangle are related as $1 : 1 : \sqrt{2}$.

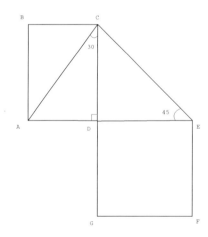

$\triangle ACD$ is a $30° - 60° - 90°$ triangle, so its sides are related as $1 : \sqrt{3} : 2$. Hence,

$$\frac{1}{2}AD \cdot CD = \frac{\sqrt{3}}{2}AD^2 = \frac{1}{2} \cdot 4\sqrt{3}, \ \sqrt{3}AD^2 = 4\sqrt{3}.$$

So, $AD = 2$, and $CD = DE = 2\sqrt{3}$. So, the area of $DEFG$ is 12. Therefore, the best answer is (E).

26.

$$\frac{3}{4} - \frac{2}{3} = \frac{3 \times 3 - 2 \times 4}{12}$$
$$= \frac{9-8}{12} = \frac{1}{12}, \text{ and}$$
$$\frac{1}{\frac{1}{12}} = 12.$$

Therefore, the best answer is (E).

27. Let the distance between A and B be a and the distance between B and C be b. Then, $a + b = 150$, and $a = 5b$. To find out b, substitute the latter into the former to obtain that $6b = 150$. So, $b = 25$, and the best answer is (D).

28. The key is to remember that ray R has completed one revolution around the origin. One revolution with a radius of 1 results in a circumference of 2π. Then, it is best to proceed by elimination. I is not true because this angle is in the third quadrant, and it is given that ray R has completed one revolution around the origin. II points to the angle in the second quadrant. III simplifies to $3\pi + \frac{\pi}{4} < x < 3\pi + \frac{\pi}{2}$. Now, it is clear that III is the only answer. Therefore, the best answer is (C).

29. To find the percent of original sum spent, one may focus on the proportion of M remaining after each expenditure. Suppose the professor received just 100 dollars. After his university collected 25 dollars, the professor was left with 75 dollars. Then, to purchase lab equipment he spent $\frac{1}{5}$ (20%) of the remaining 75 dollars, and he was left with only $75 - \frac{75}{5} = 60$ dollars. So, the professor was left with just 60 dollars from the original 100 dollars, i.e. he spent 40 percent of the grant. A quicker solution follows if one converts percents to fractions to see that the professor was left with just

$$0.75 \times 0.80 \times M = \frac{3}{4} \times \frac{4}{5} \times M = \frac{3}{5}M = 0.6M$$

dollars, which implies $0.4 (= 40\%)$ of the original sum was spent. Therefore, the best answer is (B).

30. The key is to realize that the distance between the points is of no importance. After 9 hours of flight time, plane I covers $\frac{9}{15} = \frac{3}{5}$ of the route with $\frac{2}{5}$ of the route remaining. If plane II picks up where plane I left off, then it will cover $\frac{2}{5}$ of the route in $\frac{2}{5}10 = 4$ hours. Therefore, the best answer is (E).

31. The key is to know that the total wealth of \$60 did not change during the game, it was only redistributed among the players. Let G, D, and M be the 'wealth' of each player at the end of the game. $G = 12 + D$ and $G = \frac{1}{2}M$. Since the name of the game is zero sum, $G + (G - 12) + 2G = 60$ and $G = 18$. So, Gaby lost \$2 or won -2 dollars. Therefore, the best answer is (B).

32. Since the average inventory is $\frac{y}{2}$ per month at \$0.5 per month, the total annual inventory cost is

$$12 \times 0.5 \times \frac{y}{2} = 3y.$$

Therefore, the best answer is (B).

33. The numerator is

$$
\begin{aligned}
1 + \frac{xy}{z^2} &= 1 + \frac{\frac{z}{2} \times \frac{3z}{4}}{z^2} \\
&= 1 + \frac{\frac{3z^2}{8}}{z^2} \\
&= 1 + \frac{3}{8} = \frac{11}{8}.
\end{aligned}
$$

The denominator is $\frac{5z}{4}$,

$$\frac{\frac{11}{8}}{\frac{5z}{4}} = \frac{11}{10z}.$$

Therefore, the best answer is (A).

34. Clearly, the answers (C), (D), (E) are too large to approximate y since $50^2 = 2,500$. (B) is not accurate enough since $20^2 = 400$, $(-14)^2 = 196$. Always, an even power of a negative number is positive. Therefore, the best answer is (A).

35. First, notice that the fraction of useable clips turned out to be smaller than it had been initially believed. So, the actual price paid was higher. To solve the problem, it is helpful to realize that the number of clips in a lot can be any. So, pick one which is suitable for doing the calculations. Here, the convenient number of clips in the lot is the one which is divisible by both 5 and 7. Since 5 and 7 are primes, the easiest number that is divisible by the both of them is 35, their least common multiple. So, if there were 35 clips in the lot, then at \$3 per admissible clip the total dollar amount paid for the lot was

$$3 \times \frac{5}{7} \times 35 = 3 \times 25 = 75,$$

whereas the actual price per useable clip was

$$\frac{75}{35 \times \frac{3}{5}} = \frac{25}{7} = 3\frac{4}{7}$$

dollars. Therefore, the best answer is (B).

36. Marie-Ann's savings of \$62.5 is just the number of megabytes of RAM n she purchased times the price differential of \$1.25 per megabyte, i.e. $1.25n = 62.5$. To compute $n = \frac{62.5}{1.25}$, convert the numbers into fractions:

$$\begin{aligned}\frac{62.5}{1.25} &= \frac{60 + 2 + \frac{1}{2}}{\frac{5}{4}} \\ &= \frac{(60 + 2 + \frac{1}{2})4}{5} \\ &= 50.\end{aligned}$$

Therefore, the best answer is (B).

37. Substituting the values of x and n, we obtain that

$$\left(\frac{1}{36}\right)^{\frac{1}{2}} - \left(\frac{1}{36 - 9}\right)^{\frac{1}{3}} = \frac{1}{6} - \frac{1}{3} = -\frac{1}{6}.$$

Therefore, the best answer is (C).

38. The group needs to walk $45 - 19 = 26$ miles during the second day. So, the distance walked during the second day must grow by $x \times 100$ percent, where x is such that $26 = 19(1 + x)$. Solving for x yields that $x \approx 0.368$. Therefore, the best answer is (D).

39. Proceed by elimination. (A) is out since a is divisible by 3. (B) is out since $(ab + 3)/3 = (ab)/3 + 1$, which is divisible by 3 since a is divisible by 3. (C) is clearly out, as well as (E) since $a + 3b = 3(a/3 + b)$ is divisible by 3. $3a + b$ is not divisible by 3 since b is not divisible by 3. Therefore, the best answer is (D).

40. The key is to convert decimal expressions above to fractions. When that is done, we obtain

$$\frac{\frac{11}{30}\frac{5}{6}\frac{1}{3}}{\frac{4}{9}\frac{2}{3}\frac{1}{8}} = \frac{11}{4} = 2.75.$$

To obtain the above, notice that most of the numbers above can be derived from $\frac{1}{3}$.

Numerator :

$$
\begin{aligned}
0.3667 &\approx 0.3 + 0.0667 \\
&\approx \frac{3}{10} + 2 \times 0.0333 \\
&\approx \frac{9}{30} + 2 \times \frac{1}{30} = \frac{11}{30},
\end{aligned}
$$

$$
\begin{aligned}
0.8333 &\approx \frac{8}{10} + \frac{1}{30} \\
&\approx \frac{24}{30} + \frac{1}{30} \\
&\approx \frac{25}{30} \approx \frac{5}{6},
\end{aligned}
$$

$$
0.3333 \approx \frac{1}{3}.
$$

denominator:

$$
\begin{aligned}
0.4444 &\approx 2 \times 0.2222 \\
&\approx 2\left(\frac{0.6667}{3}\right) \\
&\approx \frac{2}{3}(2 \times 0.3333) \\
&\approx \frac{2}{3} \times \frac{2}{3} \approx \frac{4}{9},
\end{aligned}
$$

$$
0.6667 \approx \frac{2}{3}, \text{ and } 0.125 = \frac{1}{8}.
$$

Simplifying the fraction in the beginning of the solution, we obtain that the best answer is (D).

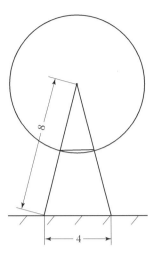

41. The altitude of the isosceles triangle formed by the support legs is $\sqrt{64 - 4} = 2\sqrt{15}$. From similarity of triangles, the ratio of the length between supports to the length of the reinforcement bar is equal to the ratio of the leg to the radius of the wheel. So, the radius of the wheel is of length 4. So, the fly would sit $2(2 + \sqrt{15})$ centimeters high above the surface. Therefore, the best answer is (E).

42. One way to think about the problems is in terms of fixed, variable costs, and a correction term to the fixed cost. An airline charges a variable cost of $\frac{e}{3}$ euros for each flight leg. Since n tickets give $2n$ flight legs, the variable cost of n trips is $2n\frac{n}{3}$. The airline also charges a fixed cost of e euros for the first leg. This price of e euros includes both the fixed and the variable cost for this leg. So, we have to subtract the correction term of $\frac{e}{3}$ euros of variable costs for the first leg. In total, the price of n tickets is the variable cost for $2n$ legs plus a fixed cost for the first leg minus a correction term:

$$2n\frac{e}{3} + e - \frac{e}{3} = \frac{2ne}{3} + \frac{3e}{3} - \frac{e}{3}$$
$$= \frac{2ne + 2e}{3}.$$

We provide another solution below. n round-trips make for $2n$ flight legs, the first of which is priced at e euros, and the rest $2n - 1$ are priced at $\frac{e}{3}$ euros. So, the total cost of all n tickets is

$$e + \frac{(2n - 1)e}{3} = \frac{2e + 2ne}{3}.$$

Therefore, the best answer is (B).

43. The statement $uvw \neq 0$ means that none of the numbers u, v, and w is equal to 0. Let us parse the statement 'u percent of v percent of w is k' sequentially. u percent of v is just $\frac{u}{100}v$. Then, $\frac{u}{100}v$ percent of w is just

$$\frac{\frac{u}{100}v}{100}w.$$

The fraction above simplifies to $\frac{uvw}{10000}$, which equals k. This leads to the answer given in (C)

$$w = \frac{10,000k}{uv}.$$

Therefore, the best answer is (C).

44. One can substitute 1 in 1,000 by u, 1 in 10,000 by v, and 1 in 10 by w, stack the numbers in a table for addition, and observe that the units' digit in N is 0 and the tens is w. Therefore, the best answer is (E).

45. Intuitively, a 20 percent increase in water level from level m to 12 meters means that $m = 10$. Hence, $12 - m = 12 - 10 = 2$. Mathematically, $\frac{12-m}{m} = \frac{1}{5}$, $60 = 6m$, $m = 10$, and $12 - m = 2$. Therefore, the best answer is (A).

46.

$$\sqrt{\frac{1}{36} + \frac{1}{64}} = \sqrt{\frac{36 + 64}{6^2 \cdot 8^2}}$$
$$= \frac{10}{48} = \frac{5}{24}.$$

Therefore, the best answer is (D).

47. We need to find the pair for which $y^3 > x$. Proceed by elimination to obtain that that in the pair $(57, 4)$, $4^3 = 64 > 57$. Therefore, the best answer is (C).

48. The key is to use the properties of two parallel lines with a secant. To find the measure of y, we need to relate L_1 and L_2. If L_1 were parallel to L_2, then $y = 120°$ from the properties of two parallels and a secant. Given the information in this question, we cannot infer that $L_1 \| L_2$. Therefore, the best answer is (E).

49. Let the side of the smallest triangle be s. Then, its area is

$$\frac{1}{2}s\sqrt{s^2 - \frac{s^2}{4}} = \frac{\sqrt{3}}{4}s^2.$$

Since all the triangles are equilateral, the side of the largest triangle is $4s$. Its area is

$$\frac{1}{2}4s\sqrt{16s^2 - 4s^2} = 4\sqrt{3}s^2.$$

Dividing the area of the smallest triangle by the largest, we get $\frac{1}{16}$.

For a simple counting argument, see the figure below.

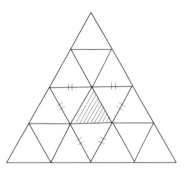

16 equilateral triangles are obtained by connecting the midpoints of the sides of the outer triangles and, then, repeating the same procedures once again for each of the four thus constructed triangles. It follows from this procedure that all 16 triangles are equal by equality of their sides. Therefore, the best answer is (A).

50. Here, it is fairly easy to enumerate k. For example,

$$(102, 201), (112, 211), \quad \ldots \quad , (192, 291),$$
$$\ldots \quad , (899, 998),$$

which is the total of 80 pairs. Each hundred has 10 numbers with this property, and there are 8 hundreds which satisfy the property and the magnitude requirement. Therefore, the best answer is (D).

51. It is possible to use two methods to solve the question. One method is general, the other involves a shortcut. The shortcut is based on realizing that in questions about fraction of a total original numbers are immaterial as long as they are scaled using the same proportion. To illustrate this point, let us find the total number of calls answered between 10 am and 11 am; it is $\frac{60}{4.5}$ - not an impossible, but an inconvenient computation. To make computing easier, one can scale the numbers multiplying all service times by 2 to obtain $3, 9$ and 10 as an average service time per call during each hour between 9 am and 12 pm, respectively. Now, we can choose a convenient calling period, say, 90 minutes. So, each calling period contains $\frac{90}{3} = 30, \frac{90}{9} = 10$, and $\frac{90}{10} = 9$ calls per service period. So, the ratio of inquiries answered during the first service period to the total number of inquiries is $\frac{30}{30+10+9} = \frac{30}{49}$. One can also review general computations below.

The fraction required in the answer is the ratio of calls answered between 9 and 10 to the total number of calls answered during the three hour period. The total number of calls is equal to

$$
\begin{aligned}
\frac{60}{1.5} + \frac{60}{4.5} + \frac{60}{5} &= \frac{60}{\frac{3}{2}} + \frac{60}{\frac{9}{2}} + 12 \\
&= \frac{60 \times 2}{3} + \frac{60 \times 2}{9} + 12 \\
&= 40 + \frac{40}{3} + 12 \\
&= 65\frac{1}{3} = \frac{196}{3}.
\end{aligned}
$$

Since 40 calls are answered between 9 and 10, the fraction required is

$$
\begin{aligned}
\frac{40}{\frac{196}{3}} &= \frac{40 \times 3}{196} \\
&= \frac{3 \times 4 \times 10}{4 \times 49} \\
&= \frac{30}{49}.
\end{aligned}
$$

Therefore, the best answer is (C).

52. The key is to solve the quadratic in the numerator. But, one can immediately eliminate (A) since -24 produces an undefined expression, $\frac{0}{0}$, if 24 is the root of the quadratic. The numerator of the fraction factors in $(x - 10)(x + 24)$. So, the second term in the product cancels. To factor the quadratic in the numerator, note that the product of the roots is -240 and the difference of the roots is 14. Solving two equations with two unknowns will yield the roots of the quadratic. Therefore, the best answer is (E).

53. Since 1 unit of a catalyst will work for, at most, $\frac{7}{4}$ units of a chemical, $20\frac{4}{7} = \frac{144}{7}$ units of the catalyst will work for

$$
\frac{\frac{144}{7}}{\frac{4}{7}} = \frac{144 \cdot 7}{7 \cdot 4} = 36
$$

reactions. Therefore, the best answer is (C).

54. The transformations of shifting (subtracting 10) and scaling (multiplying by a constant) changes the mean of the sample in accordance with the operations performed on the data. For instance, let $x_1, \ldots, x_n$ be a sample of size n, and let a and b be two real numbers. The average, $\bar{x}$, (arithmetic mean) of the sample is computed as

$$\bar{x} = \frac{x_1 + \ldots + x_n}{n} = \frac{1}{n} \sum_{i=1}^{n} x_i.$$

Suppose that a and b above are the shifting and scaling factors, respectively, then the mean of the transformed data, $\bar{x}'$, is computed as

$$\begin{aligned}
\bar{x}' &= \frac{b(x_1 + a) + \ldots + b(x_n + a)}{n} \\
&= \frac{1}{n} \sum_{i=1}^{n} b(x_i + a) \\
&= b \frac{1}{n} \left(\sum_{i=1}^{n} x_i + \sum_{i=1}^{n} a \right) \\
&= b \left(\bar{x} + \frac{na}{n} \right) \\
&= b(\bar{x} + a).
\end{aligned}$$

Observing the order of transformations performed, we obtain $(15 - 10)1.5 = 7.5$. Therefore, the best answer is (D).

55. The total number of cars of all three models is $19 + 17 + 15 = 51$, and $\frac{51}{3} = 17$. So, there must be 17 cars in each showroom. A quicker way to arrive at 17 is just to subtract 2 from 19 and add it to 15. Since each model must be represented by at least a single car in every show room, the largest number of model A cars can be 15. Therefore, the best answer is (C).

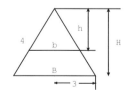

56.

Please see the drawing of the cross-section above. If H is the altitude of the triangular cross-section, then $H = \sqrt{16 - 9} = \sqrt{7}$ by the property of isosceles triangles. If h is the height of the cross-section empty of water, then $h = \sqrt{7} - 1$.

By similarity of triangles,

$$\frac{b}{B} = \frac{h}{H},$$

$$\frac{b}{6} = \frac{\sqrt{7} - 1}{\sqrt{7}},$$

$$b = \frac{6(\sqrt{7} - 1)}{\sqrt{7}}$$

$$= 6\left(1 - \frac{\sqrt{7}}{7}\right).$$

So, the total volume v empty of water is

$$v = 10 \times \frac{1}{2}bh$$

$$= 10 \times \frac{1}{2} \times 6\left(1 - \frac{\sqrt{7}}{7}\right) \times (\sqrt{7} - 1)$$

$$= 60\left(\frac{4}{7}\sqrt{7} - 1\right).$$

If V is the total volume of the triangular cylinder, and W is the volume filled with water, then $W = V - v$, and the depth, D, of the water required is

$$D = \frac{W}{\frac{1}{2}BH}.$$

$$W = V - v$$

$$= 10 \times \frac{1}{2}BH - 60\left(\frac{4}{7}\sqrt{7} - 1\right)$$

$$= 30\sqrt{7} - 60\left(4\frac{\sqrt{7}}{7} - 1\right)$$

$$= \left(\frac{210\sqrt{7}}{7} - \frac{240\sqrt{7}}{7} + 60\right)$$

$$= 60 - \frac{30\sqrt{7}}{7}.$$

From the expression given for D above,

$$
\begin{aligned}
D &= \frac{W}{\frac{1}{2}BH} \\
&= \left(60 - \frac{30}{7}\sqrt{7}\right)/3\sqrt{7} \\
&= \frac{20}{7}\sqrt{7} - \frac{10}{7} \\
&= \frac{10}{7}\left(2\sqrt{7} - 1\right)
\end{aligned}
$$

Therefore, the best answer is (D).

57. First, note that there are 51 and NOT 50 integers between and including 250 and 300. $2 \times 5 + 1 = 11$ of them are divisible by 5. Now, we have to count all the integers divisible by 3 excluding those already counted as divisible by 5 to avoid double counting. 252 is divisible by 3 since the sum of digits which compose 252 is divisible by 3. Then, similarly, 255 is divisible by 3, but it has to be excluded from this enumeration since it has already been counted as divisible by 5. So, it is possible to enumerate all the integers divisible by 3. This list contains 13 integers. So, there $13 + 11 = 24$ integers which are divisible by 3 or 5 or both. Hence, there $51 - 24 = 27$ integers which are divisible by NEITHER 3 NOR 5. Therefore, the best answer is (C).

58. We are looking for the number x such that $15 = (1-x)18$. So, $1 - x = \frac{5}{6} \approx 0.8333$ and $x \approx 1 - 0.8333 = 0.1667 \approx 0.17$ or 17%. Therefore, the best answer is (E).

59. The fastest way is to proceed by elimination. It is clear that the fraction in (C) is larger than the fraction in (E) (their denominators are the same). So, (C) is out. Multiplying the fraction in (E) by $\frac{1}{2}$, we obtain $\frac{4.5}{50}$, which is smaller than the fraction in (D). So, (D) is out. If the numerator and the denominator of (E) is divided by 5, we can see that (E) is also out since $\frac{9}{5} > 1$, the numerator of the fraction in (B). Now, only (A) and (B) remain. (A) can be reduced to $\frac{1}{50}$. Since $\frac{1}{50} < \frac{1}{20}$, (B) is out, and only (A) remains. The other way is to find the least common denominator of all fractions and compare the numerators. The least common denominator for all the fractions listed is 300. Then, from top to bottom, the numerators of the fractions above are $6, 15, 39, 162$, and 27. Therefore, the best answer is (A).

60. If the new volume is denoted by y, and if the new volume of the chamber is increased by one-half as much as the original one, then the new volume is related

to the original one as 3 to 2, i.e. the following relation must hold: $\frac{y}{1000} = \frac{3}{2}$, which implies that $y = 1500$ cubic meters. This adds 500 cubic meters of additional volume. Adding a parallelepiped addition to a side of a cube keeps two of the dimension of the parallelepiped fixed. So, if the dimensions of a parallelepiped with the volume of 500 meters cubed are $x : 10 : 10$, then $x = 5$. Therefore, the best answer is (C).

61. The experienced secretary continues typing for $\frac{800}{80} = 10$ minutes before the computer break-down, and the beginner manages to complete 300 characters in that time. So, it takes the beginner only $\frac{500}{30}$ minutes, or $\frac{500}{30 \times 60} = \frac{5}{18}$ of an hour to break even. Therefore, the best answer is (E).

62. It is clear that Mary and Jane can complete $\frac{1}{10}$ and $\frac{1}{6}$ of the manuscript in one hour, respectively. Hence, Mary can complete $\frac{5 \cdot 1}{2 \cdot 10} = \frac{1}{4}$ of the manuscript in $2\frac{1}{2}$ hours, and Jane can complete $(5/2) \cdot (1/6) = 5/12$ of the manuscript in the same time. This leaves

$$1 - \left(\frac{1}{4} + \frac{5}{12}\right) = 1 - \frac{8}{12} = 1 - \frac{2}{3} = \frac{1}{3}$$

of the manuscript for Lucy to complete. So, Lucy can type

$$\frac{\frac{1}{3}}{\frac{5}{2}} = \frac{2}{15}$$

of the manuscript per hour. Inverting the fraction above, we obtain that Lucy is capable of completing the manuscript in $7\frac{1}{2}$ hours.

Another approach is more formal. Let $m, j,$ and l be the rates in manuscripts per hour at which Mary, Jane, and Lucy are capable of typing. So, their combined rate is $m + j + l$, and since it takes $2\frac{1}{2}$ hours to complete a manuscript,

$$\frac{1}{m + j + l} = 2\frac{1}{2} = \frac{5}{2}.$$

It is also given that $m = 0.1$ and $j = \frac{1}{6}$. Substituting these values and solving for l, we obtain that $l = \frac{2}{15}$, which is the fraction of a manuscript that Lucy can type per hour. So, it takes Lucy $7\frac{1}{2}$ hours to type the whole manuscript. Therefore, the best answer is (E).

63. Since the price for each item does not change when the number of items changes, the total cost is three times less. Therefore, the best answer is (B).

64. Total landing and take-off cost of this aircraft per week is $7l$ thousand dollars. The total under-way cost is $\frac{fm}{1000}$ thousand dollars. Summing the two costs together, we obtain (B), i.e.

$$\frac{7l \times 1000}{1000} + \frac{fm}{1000} = \frac{7000l + fm}{1000}.$$

Therefore, the best answer is (B).

65. The number of items which pass initial quality control is

$$(3,500/100) \times 80 = 35 \times 80 = 2,800,$$

and $3,500 - 2,800 = 700$ require additional tests. The quantity required is $2,800 - 700 = 2,100$. Therefore, the best answer is (D).

66. First, one needs to solve for a and b. Summing $a + b = 24$ and $3b - a = 0$, we get $4b = 24$, or $b = 6$, $a = 18$. $\sqrt{18} + \frac{18}{6} = 3\sqrt{2} + 3 = 3(\sqrt{2} + 1)$. Therefore, the best answer is (C).

67. When the ratio is not given in the form $1 : \star : \star$, it is convenient to change it to this form. In this problem, the proportion $3 : 5 : 7$ needs to be changed to $1 : \frac{5}{3} : \frac{7}{3}$. Now, to obtain the largest amount of the mixture, the brewery must use the maximum amount of enzymes it has, i.e. one cubic meter, plus $\frac{5}{3}$ cubic meters of flax, plus $\frac{7}{3}$ cubic meters of barley. All in all,

$$1 \left(= \frac{3}{3} \right) + \frac{5}{3} + \frac{7}{3} = \frac{15}{3} = 5$$

cubic meters of the mixture. Therefore, the best answer is (E).

68. Problem about ratios usually become more tractable if one chooses concrete numbers which are in the ratios as given in a problem. Here, distances that the aircraft fly are related as $1 : 3 : 5$. Let us choose these distances $100, 300,$ and 500, arbitrarily, and suppose that the aircraft burns $5, 3,$ and 1 ton of fuel, respectively. Then the fuel consumption is $20, 100,$ and 500, say, miles per ton, and are related as $1 : 5 : 25$. Therefore, the best answer is (C).

69. First, one needs to determine the layer of dust on the ground from the first fall-out. Since the volcano was erupting for just two hours at the rate given in inches per 3-hour period, the fall-out for the first time was

$$\frac{2}{3} \times (2\frac{1}{4}) = \frac{2}{3} \times \frac{9}{4} = \frac{3}{2}.$$

For the second time, the eruption lasted for 9 hours, i.e. for 3 three-hour periods, and the total fall-out was $3 \times \frac{9}{4} = \frac{27}{4}$. So, the combined fall-out was

$$\frac{3}{2} + \frac{27}{4} = \frac{6 + 27}{4} = \frac{33}{4} = 8\frac{1}{4}.$$

Therefore, the best answer is (B).

70. The key is to remember that on the second day, mountain climbers were able to cover only a fraction of the distance remaining from the first day of the climb. Specifically, $\frac{2}{7}$ of the total climb was remaining after the first day. On the second day $\frac{2}{7} \times \frac{1}{5} = \frac{2}{35}$ of the total climb was covered on the second day, so on the third day the mountaineers covered

$$1 - \left(\frac{5}{7}\left[\times\frac{5}{5}\right] + \frac{2}{35}\right) = 1 - \frac{27}{35} = \frac{8}{35}.$$

Therefore, the best answer is (C).

71. Let x and y be the number of bicycles of models 1 and 2, respectively, that are repaired daily in the shop. Then, the first sentence of the problem implies that $3y - x = 3$. The second sentence yields $x - 1 = y + 2$. We get the system of two linear equations with two unknowns

$$3y - 3 = x,$$
$$y + 2 = x - 1.$$

Subtracting the bottom equation from the top one yields the expression for y:

$$2y - 5 = 1, y = 3.$$

The value of x is obtained by substituting $y = 3$ into any equation of the system, e.g. the bottom one, to obtain that $x = 6$. So, the total number of bicycles is 9. Therefore, the best answer is (D).

72. Let w be the number of women in the class, then the number of men in the class is $2w$. Each member of the class bought 10 tickets worth $5 each, all in all 50 dollars worth of tickets. Since the total ticket sales equaled $3,150$, we have that

$50 \times 3w = 3,150$. So, the number of women in the class, w, is 21. So, since there is two men for every woman in the class, (B) is the best answer; there are 42 men in the class.

73. If a particle jumps up and down at a speed of 2 seconds in either direction, it can return to the origin every 4 seconds. So Student 1 should record down 25 times of return through a period of 100 seconds. Similarly, the particle takes 6 seconds to return to the origin each time, so the list of Student 2 is 16 entries. Student 3 should have 10 entries since it takes the particle 10 seconds to return each time. Totally, there are $25 + 16 + 10 = 51$ entries in the table. Therefore, the answer is (D).

74. The percent change is computed as a fraction of the difference between the new and the old number of movies to the old number of movies.

$$\frac{1050 - 1750}{1750} = \frac{-700}{1750} = \frac{-14 \times 50}{35 \times 50} = -\frac{2}{5} = -0.4,$$

i.e. a decrease of 40 percent.

A quicker way is to compute the fraction

$$\frac{1050}{1750} = 0.6.$$

Since the value of 1750 corresponds to 100 percent, 1050 is 60 percent of 1750. So, the decrease is 40 percent. Therefore, the best answer is (E).

75. This question requires solving the system of two equations:

$$2s = n(n + 1),$$
$$s = 3n.$$

Substituting the value of s into the first equation, we obtain a quadratic equation $6n = n^2 + n$, which gives us that $n = 5$. So, $s = 3 \times 5 = 15$. Therefore, the best answer is (E).

76. Suppose a box costs one unit of value. Then, usually, 7 boxes cost 7 units of value, and now they are sold for 4 units giving the savings to a customer of 3 units. So, savings as a percent of the total purchase is

$$\frac{3}{7} \times 100 = \frac{300}{7} = 42\frac{6}{7} \approx 42.9$$

percent. Therefore, the best answer is (C).

77.

$$\frac{625}{5^3} \times 49 = \frac{5^4}{5^3} \times 49 = 5 \times 49 = 245.$$

Therefore, the best answer is (D).

78. 12 divides both 48 and 84. If the length of the side of a square is 12 inches, then $\frac{48}{12} \times \frac{84}{12} = 4 \times 7 = 28$ squares will fit in the rectangle. No other side length of the square divides both 48 and 84. Therefore, the best answer is (B).

79. If $x \blacktriangle y$ must equal 15, then $\frac{x \blacktriangle y}{5} = 3$. Note that $\frac{x \blacktriangle y}{5} = \frac{xy}{y-x}$, which must be equal to 3. The pair $(2,6)$ fits this requirement. Therefore, the best answer is (C).

80. The information in the problem leads to the equation

$$75 = \frac{3 \times 40 + 90t}{3 + t},$$

where $3 + t$ is the total number of hours spent partying. Cross-multiplying, we get that

$$3 \times 75 + 75t = 3 \times 40 + 90t, \quad 3 \times 35 = 15t,$$

and $t = 7$. So, the total time out is 10 hours. Therefore, the best answer is (D).

81. If the lengths before and after the increase are denoted s_1 and s_2, respectively, then

$$s_2 - s_1 = 7,$$
$$s_2^2 - s_1^2 = 91.$$

$s_2 + s_1 = 13$. Therefore, the best answer is (A).

82. If x is the number of gallons to be added, then $0.15 = \frac{0.75}{1+x}$, so $x = 4$. Therefore, the best answer is (A).

83. An enumeration

$$
\begin{array}{cccccc}
4 & 6 & 8 & 10 & & \\
 & 6 & 8 & 10 & 12 & \\
 & & 8 & 10 & 12 & 14 \\
 & & & 10 & 12 & 14 & 16 \\
 & & & & 12 & 14 & 16 & 18 \\
 & & & & & 14 & 16 & 18 & 20 \\
\end{array}
$$

of all consecutive four even numbers in the required range easily shows that III is impossible, and only I and II must hold. Each row of numbers above represents the product w, in which multiplication signs are omitted, e.g. $w = 6 \times 8 \times 10 \times 12$. w is a multiple of 3 if each row above contains a multiple of 3. Since every row contains either 6 or 12, w is a multiple of 3. Note that (B) and (C) should be eliminated since no integer in the second to the last row is divisible by 5. Since only three rows contain 14 (a multiple of 7), it is not necessarily true that w is a multiple of 7. Hence, III may not always hold eliminating (D) and (E), which makes (A) the answer. Therefore, the best answer is (A).

84. Since dividing $\frac{4}{5}$ by $\frac{3}{4}$ is the same as multiplying $\frac{4}{5}$ by $\frac{4}{3}$, the denominator $\frac{4}{11}\frac{\frac{4}{5}}{\frac{3}{4}}$ is reduced to $\frac{4}{11}\frac{4\times4}{5\times3} = \frac{4\times4\times4}{3\times5\times11}$. Now, we need to bring the 4 in the numerator in the original expression to denominator and send the sequence of primes $3 \times 5 \times 11$ 'upstairs to obtain $\frac{3\times5\times11}{4\times4\times4\times4} = \frac{165}{256}$.

All considerations mentioned above appear below as a sequence of operations with fractions.

$$
\frac{\frac{1}{4}}{\frac{4}{11}\frac{\frac{4}{5}}{\frac{3}{4}}} = \frac{\frac{1}{4}}{\frac{4\cdot4\cdot4}{3\cdot5\cdot11}}
$$
$$
= \frac{3\cdot5\cdot11}{4^4}
$$
$$
= \frac{165}{256}.
$$

Therefore, the best answer is (A).

85. From the bar chart below,

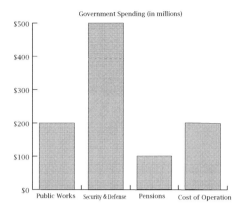

the total government spending is $200 + 500 + 100 + 200 = 1000$ million dollars.

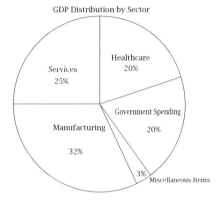

From the pie chart above, total government spending was 20% of GDP. So, the GDP was 5 billion dollars. Since the government's cost of operation was 200 million, it was $\frac{200}{5,000} \times 100 = 4$ percent of the total GDP. Therefore, the best answer is (A).

86. From the question above, total GDP is 5 billion dollars, so the dollar value of management consulting services is $\frac{5,000}{100} \times 3 = 150$ million dollars, and services account for the fourth of the total GDP, or $\frac{5,000}{4} = 1,250$ million dollars. So, the fraction of management consulting services in the total services is $\frac{150}{1,250} = 0.12$, or 12 percent. Therefore, the best answer is (C).

87. In the beginning of the year, it took $3.6 \times 10^{11} \times 10^{-6} = 3.6 \times 10^5$ seconds of computing, or 100 hours of computing. At the end of the year, it took

$$\frac{3.6 \cdot 10^{11} \cdot 10^{-1}}{2 \cdot 10^6} = \frac{1}{2} \cdot 3600 \cdot 10 = 5 \cdot 3600$$

seconds of computing, or 5 hours of computing. So, the percent decrease is

$$\frac{5 - 100}{100} = -0.95,$$

or 95 percent decrease in computing time. Therefore, the best answer is (E).

88. Since deaths exceeded births by 0.3 million, the number of Russians born in 2000 was $1.2 - 0.3 = 0.9$ million. 1 percent of the population of 167.8 million is approximately 1.7 million, of which 0.9 is, approximately, $\frac{1}{2}$, or 0.5 percent. Therefore, the best answer is (D).

89. The key is that the capacity may be any convenient quantity, say, 100 tons. Then, after its departure from Murmansk, the tanker has 50 tons of oil on board, $50 \times (3/10) = 15$ tons of which is sulphur. Since the North Sea oil contains sulphur in negligible amounts, after its departure from a North Sea terminal, the sulphur content of oil in the tanker was $15/100 = 0.15$, or 15 percent. Therefore, the best answer is (A).

90. The first thing to check is that an advertising cost per week does not fall below the operational cost of $2,000$ dollars per week. It is clearly true for weeks 1 through 3. In week 4, the advertising cost was $0.1 \cdot 4 \cdot 5,000 = 2,000$ dollars, right on the mark. So, the total advertising revenue was $\underbrace{2 \times 0.1 \times 4 \times 20,000}_{\text{first two weeks}} + 0.1 \times 4 \times 15,000 + 0.1 \times 4 \times 5,000 = 24,000$ dollars. Therefore, the best answer is (D).

91. The total distance covered by the hammer in 5 seconds is

$$\frac{1}{2}gt^2 = \frac{1}{2} \times 32.2 \times 5^2 = 402.5.$$

The distance between the roof of the building and the professor's office window is the distance that the object covered in the first 2 seconds of its flight

$$\frac{1}{2} \times 32.2 \times 2^2 = 64.4.$$

The difference $402.5 - 64.4 = 338.1$ is what the question requires. Therefore, the best answer is (D).

92. The difference is obtained from

$$440 \times \frac{8}{10} - 440 \times \frac{2}{10} = 440\left(\frac{4}{5} - \frac{1}{5}\right)$$
$$= 440 \times \frac{3}{5}$$
$$= 44 \times 2 \times 3$$
$$= 44 \times 6$$
$$= 264.$$

Therefore, the best answer is (D).

93. The new price of $\frac{1}{4}$ of a dollar for a bagel is related to x percent in the same way as the old price of $\frac{1}{5}$ of a dollar for a bagel is related to 100 percent. So, we obtain a fractional relation $\frac{\frac{1}{4}}{x} = \frac{\frac{1}{5}}{100}$, $x = \frac{5}{4} \times 100$ percent. x is the new price as a percent of the old price. So, we need to subtract 100 percent of the old price from x to obtain 25 percent.

Another way is use the definition of a percent change:

$$\frac{(1/4) - (1/5)}{1/5} = \frac{1/20}{1/5} = \frac{5}{20} = \frac{1}{4},$$

or 25%. Therefore, the best answer is (E).

94. Each interval represents a difference of 0.002, and the arrow points to the middle of the third interval between 1.044 and 1.046. Therefore, the best answer is (D).

95. Dividing by 3, we obtain the sequence $20, 21, 24, 30$, and 45. Respectively, their prime number decomposition is $20 = 2 \times 2 \times 5$, $21 = 3 \times 7$, $24 = 2^3 \times 3$, $30 = 2 \times 3 \times 5$, $45 = 3^2 \times 5$. It is clear now that only 30 has 3 distinct primes in its decomposition, the rest of the numbers have just 2 distinct primes. Therefore, the best answer is (D).

96.

$$
\begin{aligned}
4^{n+1} \cdot 25^n &= 4 \cdot (100)^n \\
&= 4 \cdot \left(10^2\right)^n \\
&= 4 \cdot 10^{2n} \\
&= 400,000 \\
&= 4 \cdot 10^5.
\end{aligned}
$$

So, $2n = 5$, $n = 2.5$. Therefore, the best answer is (C).

97. Since running an ad on a quarter of the front page costs 10 thousand, and the cost of the same area ad on the remaining 9 pages is 2 thousand, the total revenue is $10 + 2 \cdot 9 = 28$ thousand dollars. Therefore, the best answer is (C).

98. The average speed is total distance divided by total time. So, the speed is $\frac{d+500}{72+h}$

kilometers per hour. $72 + h$ hours is $\frac{72+h}{24}$ days, which leads to the answer

$$\frac{d+500}{\frac{72+h}{24}} = \frac{24(d+500)}{72+h}.$$

Therefore, the best answer is (A).

99. $A = \sqrt{3}a^2$ can be manipulated into $a = \sqrt{\frac{A}{\sqrt{3}}}$. So, the question requires to find the value of the difference $\sqrt{\frac{625\sqrt{3}}{\sqrt{3}}} - \sqrt{\frac{196\sqrt{3}}{\sqrt{3}}}$, which is simplified to $\sqrt{625} - \sqrt{196} = 25 - 14 = 11$. Therefore, the best answer is (C).

100. The key is to realize that the total number of customers served by the chain could be any computationally convenient number. Suppose the chain serves 100 customers. 60 of them order a raw fish dish, and $\frac{60}{4} = 15$ of them order sashimi. So, 15 percent of all customers order sashimi. Therefore, the best answer is (C).

101. It is useful to consider two methods. The first one is based on the fact that for any sequence of numbers, the sum of their differences from their arithmetic mean is zero. Given that each score is distinct, the sum of differences of scores from their arithmetic mean is at least $(60-50)+(59-50)+(58-50)+(57-50)+(56-50) = 10+9+8+7+6 = 40$. So, the lowest score x is such that $40 + (x-50) = 0$. This equation implies that $x = 10$. Another solution follows below.

The total number of scores received by 6 students is $50 \times 6 = 300$. The lowest possible score is obtained when the top 5 students scored the highest distinct scores. So, the lowest score is $300 - (60+59+58+57+56) = 300 - 290 = 10$. Therefore, the best answer is (C).

102. $\frac{5}{4}k = 1$ means that $k = \frac{4}{5}$, and after substituting the value of k, we have that $\frac{1}{k+5} = \frac{1}{\frac{4}{5}+5} = \frac{1}{\frac{29}{5}} = \frac{5}{29}$. Therefore, the best answer is (A).

103. The key is not to double-count students taking both courses. Since the number of students in the English Lit. and the number of students in the English Comp. include those who take both, we need to subtract them from the total number of English Lit. and English Comp. students, i.e. $160 + 200 - 120 = 240$. Therefore, the best answer is (E).

104. The answer requires the knowledge of an algebraic identity that $a^2 - b^2 = (a-b)(a+b)$. With this in mind, $(226)^2 - (225)^2 = 1 \times (226+225) = 451$. If one cannot

recall the identity, it is still possible to eliminate the majority of wrong answers by subtracting the square of the unit digit of the first number from the square of the unit digit of the second number: $6^2 - 5^2 = 36 - 26 = 11$. So, the unit digit of the answer is 1. (A) is a catch since the answer is at least 225. The expression in question is always bigger than $226 \times 225 - 225 \times 225 = 225 \times (226 - 225) = 225$. So, here it is possible to eliminate everything but (E). Therefore, the best answer is (E).

105. The average rate of arrival during the day is the ratio of the total number of customers who arrive at the bank during the day to the total number of hours that the bank remains open. The rate of arrival during the morning is given in customers per unit of time. So, multiplying the rate by hours will yield the number of customers arriving to the bank in the morning. The same is true for the afternoon. Hence, the total number of customers who arrive to the bank during the day is $r_1 t_1 + r_2 t_2$, and the average rate of arrival for the day is $\frac{r_1 t_1 + r_2 t_2}{t_1 + t_2}$. Therefore, the best answer is (C).

106. The key is to choose a convenient number. Suppose a store stocks 120 pairs of shoes of size 9 and 9.5. Then it stocks 60 pairs of shoes of size 8, and 20 shoes of size 10. So, size 8 shoes is $\frac{60}{20+60+120+120} = \frac{6}{32} = \frac{3}{16} = 0.1875$, or 18.75% of the total number of shoes stored. Therefore, the best answer is (D).

107. We proceed by elimination, first choosing the specific values of a, b, c, and d, for which $ad = bc$ holds. For $a = 2, d = 5, b = 1, c = 10$, (C) is not true. Therefore, the best answer is (C).

108. The answer depends on knowing a simple algebraic identity that

$$a^2 - b^2 = (a - b)(a + b).$$

To apply the above formula, the expression

$$\frac{u^2 - 25}{4v} = \frac{(u - 5)(u + 5)}{4v} = \frac{u - 5}{8}$$

is immediately simplified to

$$\frac{u + 5}{v} = \frac{1}{2}, u = \frac{v}{2} - 5 = \frac{v - 10}{2}$$

Therefore, the best answer is (A).

109. We can easily check that the statement I $2a^3 - b^2 = 2 \cdot (-2)^3 - 2^2 = 2(-8) - 4 = -20$
holds, and the statement II $2a^2 - b^3 = 2(-2)^2 - 2^3 = 0$ holds, and the statement
$a^2 - 2b^3 = (-2)^2 - 2^4 = -12 \neq -4$ does not hold when $a = -2$ and $b = 2$.
Therefore, the best answer is (B).

110. Please see the figure below.

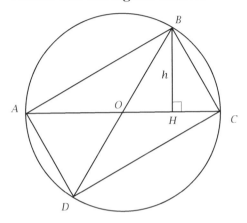

First, note that $\triangle ABC = \triangle CDA$. This follows from the fact that points B, O, and
D lie on the same line, which allows to split the above-mentioned triangles into
pairs of triangles ABO, BOC and AOD, DOC and see that the first triangle in each
pair is equal to the second triangle in the other pair, and vice versa. So, it is
sufficient to focus on $\triangle ABC$.

The length of the altitude h of $\triangle ABC$ is obtained from the expression $A = \frac{1}{2}bh$
for the area A of $\triangle ABC$.

$$h = (2 \cdot 18\sqrt{3})/12 = 3\sqrt{3}.$$

Then, the area of $\triangle BOC$ is $\frac{1}{2} \cdot 6 \cdot 3\sqrt{3} = 9\sqrt{3}$, and

$$
\begin{aligned}
\mathbf{A}(\triangle ODC) &= \mathbf{A}(\triangle OBA) \qquad \mathbf{A} \text{ denotes area} \\
&= \mathbf{A}(\triangle ABC) - \mathbf{A}(\triangle OBC) \\
&= 18\sqrt{3} - 9\sqrt{3} \\
&= 9\sqrt{3}.
\end{aligned}
$$

Therefore, the best answer is (B).

111. $13.5 = 3 \times 4.5$ and $27 = 3 \times 9$, so it is convenient to write $\frac{13.5}{100} \times \frac{2}{27}$ as

$$\frac{2 \times 3 \times 4.5}{3 \times 9 \times 100},$$

so that the cancellations can be easily performed to obtain 0.01. Therefore, the best answer is (B).

112. The area of the figure is the area of three semi-circles plus the area of a triangle. So, the volume of the figure is

$$5 \times \left(3 \cdot \frac{1}{2} \cdot \pi \cdot 20^2 + \frac{1}{2} \cdot 40 \cdot 20\sqrt{3}\right).$$

After doing some algebra, the expression above simplifies to $3,000\pi + 2,000\sqrt{3}$. Therefore, the best answer is (B).

113. Let s be the price at which the retailer sells the product, c be the cost of the product to producer, p_1 be the monetary value of producer's profits, and p_2 be the value of warehouse plus retailer's profits. So,

$$s = c + p_1 + p_2.$$

We need to obtain

$$\frac{p_1 + p_2}{c} = \frac{p_1}{c} + \frac{p_2}{c}.$$

It is given that $p_1/c = 0.2$ and $p_2/s = 0.2$ since both the producer's and the retailer's mark-up is 20 percent. To find p_2/c, we expand $p_2 = 0.2s = (1/5)(c + p_1 + p_2)$ and divide both sides by c to obtain

$$5(p_2/c) = 1 + p_1/c + p_2/c, \quad 4(p_2/c) = 1 + 0.2,$$

and after a little algebra, $p_2/c = 0.3$. So, the quantity required is 0.5, or 50 percent.

A shorter way to obtain the result is to start with

$$s = c + p_1 + p_2 = c + 0.2c + 0.2s.$$

Hence,

$$0.8s = 1.2c, \quad s = \frac{6}{5} \times \frac{5}{4} = \frac{3}{2}c,$$

or the sale price is 50 greater than the cost, so the profits are 50 percent of the cost.

Yet, another way is to set $c = 100$. Then, the warehouse obtains the item for 120, and since retailer's profit margin is 20 percent on *the sale price s*, $s = 120 + 0.2s$, $s = (5/4)120 = 150$. Clearly, the profits are 50 percent of the cost. Therefore, the best answer is (C).

114. Let s and d denote single and dual degree students, respectively. Then, we can write down the information given in the problem in terms of s and d: $s + d = 360$ and $\frac{d}{s} = \frac{7}{11}$. Since we are looking for s, it is useful to express d in terms of s as $d = 360 - s$ and substitute this expression into the fraction. Then,

$$\frac{360 - s}{s} = \frac{7}{11}.$$

Cross-multiplying, we have that

$$11(360 - s) = 7s, 11 \times 360 = 18s, s = 220.$$

Therefore, the best answer is (D).

115. It is best to summarize the information of this problem in a table. Let B and O be the number of yachts with blue and orange sails, and let V and H be the number of yachts with vertical and horizontal stripes on their sails. Suppose that the fleet has 100 yachts.

Totals	$V = 42$	$H =$
$B = 70$	$\frac{3}{10} \times 70 = 21$	
$O =$		

The next table gives all the additional information that can be filled in given the assumption that there are 100 yachts in the fleet.

Totals	$V = 42$	$H = 58$
$B = 70$	$\frac{3}{10} \times 70 = 21$	49
$O = 30$	21	9

Therefore, the best answer is (C).

116. If the units position of an integer is either 2 or 7, then it produces a remainder of 2 when divided by 5. Call any integer generated by the program x. Then, $x = 5k + 2$ for any positive integer k. It is clear that when x is divided by 10, the result is NOT an integer. Therefore, the best answer is (C).

117. u and v are of opposite signs and can take a numerical value of 1 or 7. So, their sum is either 6 or -6, and $6^3 = 216$, $(-6)^3 = -216$. Therefore, the best answer is (E).

118. Three-digit numbers yielding 1 in the remainder when divided by 100 are $101, 201, ..., 901$. Of the numbers $100, 200, ..., 900$, only those which contain 2, and 3 in their prime number decomposition are divisible by 60. These numbers are $300, 600$, and 900. Therefore, the best answer is (D).

119. 4 pairs of socks purchased in a package is $(15/20) \times 100 = 75$ percent of the price of 4 pairs of socks purchased separately. So, buying in a package is 25 percent cheaper.

Differently, a pair of socks bought in a package costs $15/4$ dollars. $15/4$ is

$$\frac{15/4}{5} = \frac{15}{20} = \frac{3}{4}$$

of the price paid for a pair of socks purchased separately. Hence, buying in a package is 25 percent cheaper. Therefore, the best answer is (D).

120. First, note that a quarter contains three months and $52/4 = 13$ weeks. It is given that a single student is capable of updating

$$250 \times \frac{25}{13} \times \frac{1}{100}$$

questions per week. So, Manhattan Review needs

$$\frac{250}{13 \times 250 \times \frac{25}{13} \times \frac{1}{100}} = \frac{100}{25} = 4$$

students on average. Therefore, the best answer is (C).

121.

$$\begin{aligned}
9.09m &= 99,999 - 90,909 \\
&= 9,090, \\
m &= \frac{909 \cdot 1000}{909} \\
&= 1,000.
\end{aligned}$$

Therefore, the best answer is (A).

122. The height of the inclined section is $\sqrt{1 - 0.64} = 0.6$ meters. So, we can infer the total number of inclined and flat section by calculating $\frac{5.4}{0.6} = 9$. Since the length of an inclined section plus the length of a flat section is 1.8, the total length from point P to point Q is $9 \times 1.8 - 16.2$ meters. Therefore, the best answer is (E). Another way to solve it is to determine which one of the five answer choices is a multiple of 1.8, the sum of the widths of an inclined section and a flat section. This leaves us choices C and E. in C, $10.8 = 6 \times 1.8$. Assuming there are 6 continuous steps, since the dam's height is 5.4, we can conclude the height of each step is $5.4/6 = 0.9$. Since 0.9 can not be the height of a side in a triangle with two other sides of 1 and 0.8. Therefore (E) is the correct answer.

123. The difference in annual payments is $\frac{1}{2} = 5.75 - 5.25$ of a percent. Since each payment occurs every six months, the difference in payment is a quarter of a percent, i.e. $168 \cdot \frac{1}{4} = 42$ dollars. Therefore, the best answer is (B).

124. The key to solution here is to realize that the price of a ticket in each class is a multiple of the economy class fare. If x is the price of a ticket in the economy class, then the prices of tickets in the business and the first class are $2\frac{1}{4}x (= \frac{9}{4}x)$ and $3\frac{1}{2}x (= \frac{7}{2}x)$, respectively. Knowing that the average price of tickets is $3,000$, we can set up a simple equation in terms of x,

$$\frac{x + \frac{9}{4}x + \frac{7}{2}x}{3} = 3000.$$

Equivalently,

$$x + \frac{9}{4}x + \frac{7}{2}x = 9000, \quad \frac{27}{4}x = 9000,$$

and after more algebra

$$x = \frac{4 \times 9 \times 1000}{3 \times 9} = \frac{4}{3} \times 1000.$$

To find the price of the business class ticket, we need to multiply the value of x, we have obtained in the previous line, by $\frac{9}{4}$,

$$\frac{4}{3} \times \frac{9}{4} \times 1000 = 3000.$$

Therefore, the best answer is (D).

125. This question may be solved by elimination. (A) is a sum of two even integers, which is even. So is (B). (C) is even since an even (and odd) multiple of an even integer is even, and subtracting an even integer 2 does not change the parity either. For (D), see the sentence above. Therefore, the best answer is (E).

126. The answers (A), (C), and (D) are fairly easy computationally since 5, 10, and 11, if multiplied by 1.1, will yield 5.5, 11, and 12.1, respectively. To eliminate (E) is not trivial since one needs to notice that $69 \times 0.1 = 6.9$ and $6.9 + 69 = 75.9$. So, only (B) remains. Therefore, the best answer is (B).

127. Please see the figure below for notation.

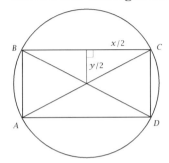

From the figure above, the Pythagorean theorem and the perimeter of $ABCD$ provide us with a system of two equations

$$\frac{x^2}{4} + \frac{y^2}{4} = 2(7.5)^2,$$
$$2x + 2y = 60.$$

After simplifying, we have that

$$x^2 + y^2 = 2(15)^2,$$
$$x + y = 30.$$

After substituting the value of $y = 30 - x$ into the top equation, we have that

$$x^2 + (30 - x)^2 = 450,$$

and after simplifying

$$
\begin{aligned}
2x^2 - 2 \cdot 30x + 450 &= 2 \times (x^2 - 2 \cdot 15x + 15^2) \\
&= 2 \times (x - 15)^2 \\
&= 0.
\end{aligned}
$$

So, both roots of the quadratic are $x = 15$ and $y = 30 - x = 15$, and the area of $ABCD$ is 225. Therefore, the best answer is (B).

128. It follows from the formulation of the problem that $w < 24$, so the train was moving for $24 - w$ hours. Its average speed for the whole time along the way was maintained at $v = \frac{(24-w)z}{24}$, and it easily follows that $z = \frac{24v}{24-w}$, where z is the speed of the train during the time when it was moving. Therefore, the best answer is (D).

129. One can just count. There are 20 integers between 37 and 57, including 57. Half of them are even. Therefore, the best answer is (D).

130. Note that both numbers are powers of primes. So, the greatest power of a prime that occurs in both numbers divides both numbers. The greatest power of 5 that occurs in both numbers is 2, and the greatest power of 11 is one. Therefore, the best answer is (B).

131. $\frac{7}{12}$ of 1.52 is just $\frac{7}{12}$ times 1.52. Converting 1.52 into a fraction, we have that

$$
\begin{aligned}
\frac{7}{12}(1.52) &= \frac{7}{12}\left(1 + \frac{52}{100}\right) \\
&= \frac{7}{12} + \frac{4 \cdot 7 \cdot 13}{4 \cdot 12 \cdot 25} \\
&= \frac{7 \cdot 25}{12 \cdot 25} + \frac{7 \cdot 13}{12 \cdot 25} \\
&= \frac{7 \cdot 38}{12 \cdot 25} \\
&= \frac{7 \cdot 2 \cdot 19}{2 \cdot 6 \cdot 25} \\
&= \frac{133}{150}.
\end{aligned}
$$

Therefore, the best answer is (C).

132. If the device was losing 10 centimeters for every 15 meters, then we need to know how many 15-meter intervals there are in 1800 meters. Conveniently, $1800/15 = 120$. So, at the end of the bridge, the device was off by 1200 centimeters, or 12 meters. Since the device underestimated the distance, the length of the bridge, according to the device, was $1800 - 12 = 1788$ meters. Therefore, the best answer is (E).

133. $u = \frac{1}{81}, v = \frac{1}{3}$, and $w = \frac{1}{9}$. Therefore, the best answer is (B).

134. Suppose it costs a dollar to hire an MA student, so it costs 2 dollars to hire an MBA. Then the total cost of hiring is $2 \cdot 140 + 40 = 320$ dollars, and the cost of hiring of the students with MA degrees is 40 dollars. So, the cost of hiring all MA's is $\frac{40}{320} = \frac{1}{8} = 0.125$ or 12.5 percent. Therefore, the best answer is (B).

135. Given that the pool is rectangular, the equation for its perimeter is $200 = 2w + 2(w + 20)$, where w is the width of the pool. It follows that $w = 40$ and $l = 60$, where l denotes the length. So, the volume of the pool is $3 \times 40 \times 60 = 7,200$ cubic meters. Therefore, the best answer is (C).

136. After dividing the numerator and denominator by 4, we obtain the ratio

$$\frac{u^2 - 5u + 6}{u - 3} = \frac{(u - 3)(u - 2)}{u - 3}.$$

Since, $u \neq 3$, we obtain $u - 2$. Therefore, the best answer is (D).

137. If P is the price of the boat, then $1.07P = 6,885.45$. This eliminates answers (D) and (E) since the numbers there are bigger than the amount Gary paid. (A) can also be eliminated since $7 \times 4 = 28$, and its units digit is 8 whereas the right most digit of the amount that Gary paid is a 5. What's left is the brute computational force concentrated on the tip of the number 2 pencil. For our purposes, it is enough to pretend that 1.07 is really just 107. So, $1.07 \times 6335 = 6,778.45$, and (B) is eliminated. Therefore, the best answer is (C).

138. The biggest number of boxes fit is obtained by placing the lowest dimension of the box, 2 meters, against the largest dimension of a container, 20 meters. So, the length of the container can allow for 10 boxes, and the width of the container allows for 2 boxes to be fit, and the height of the container fits just one box. Hence, the total number of boxes that fit in a single container is $10 \cdot 2 \cdot 1 = 20$. Therefore, the best answer is (B).

139. To find the right answer in this problem, one needs to work out the numerator only. $1 - \left(\frac{5}{6}\right)^2 = \frac{6^2}{6^2} - \frac{5^2}{6^2}$. The numerator is $6^2 - 5^2 = (6 - 5)(6 + 5) = 11$, and $11^2 = 121$. Therefore, the best answer is (D).

140. Since u is strictly less than v, then $w > 1$. Therefore, the best answer is (A).

141. The correct answer is (D). The probability of drawing blue as the first ball is 5/12. The probability of drawing the second ball as green given that the first ball drawn was blue is 4/11. The probability of drawing the third ball as yellow given that the first ball was blue and the second green is 3/10. The product is the probability of drawing blue, green, and yellow in that order.

142.   The correct answer is C). There are two possibilities: drawing a white ball from the first bag and a black ball from the second bag or drawing a black ball from the first bag and a white ball from the second bag. Drawing a white ball from the first bag has probability 3/7, black from the second bag 5/7, giving 15/49 for that scenario. The other possibility is black from the first bag (4/7) and white from the second (2/7) for a probability of 8/49. The sum gives the total probability.

143.   The correct answer is (E). The probability of rolling an odd prime is 1/3, multiplied by the probability of drawing a blue ball from Box I (3/5) gives 1/5. Adding that to the probability of not rolling an odd prime (2/3) times the probability of drawing a blue ball from Box II (5/8): $5/12 + 1/5 = 37/60$.

144.   The correct answer is (C). Six people can be seated around a round table in 5! ways. There are 2 ways that the two unwelcome people could sit next to the person in question and 3! ways of arranging the other three. This is subtracted from the base case of 5!, giving the result of 108.

145.   The correct answer is (E). $_{12}C_4$ is the number of ways that 4 marbles can be drawn from 12. $_5C_2$ is the number of ways that 2 blue marbles can be drawn from the 5. $_4C_2$ is the number of ways that 2 purple marbles can be drawn from the 4. The probability of drawing 2 purple and 2 blue is $(_5C_2)(_4C_2)/_{12}C_4$. Using complementarity, subtract the result from 1 to get the probability of <u>not</u> drawing 2 blue and 2 purple marbles.

146.   The correct answer is (A). The first number must be chosen, and therefore the probability for that event must be 1. The probability that the second number is different from the first is 9/10 because there are 9 numbers different than the first one chosen. The probability that the third number is different from the first and second is 8/10. The probabilities are independent so the probability that all 3 numbers are different is the product $1 \times 9/10 \times 8/10 = 18/25$.

147.   The correct answer is (B). $_8C_4$ is the number of ways the 4 Republicans can be chosen, $_6C_3$ is the number of ways the 3 Democrats can be chosen, and $_4C_2$ is the number of ways the 2 Independents can be chosen. The product gives the total number.

148.   The correct answer is (D). There are 4 possibilities for one-color flags, 12 for two-color flags, and 24 each for three- and four-color flags for a total of 64.

149. The correct answer is (C). The probability that he misses the first two times is $(2/5)^2$ and the probability that he hits the third time is $3/5$. The product gives the probability for hitting the bull's-eye for the first time on the third throw.

150. The correct answer is (C). The probability that the family does not win on the first drawing is $37/40$ and $12/13$ on the second. The product gives the probability that it does not win either time, $111/130$. Using complementarity, the probability that it wins at least one prize is $1 - 111/130$.

Chapter 4

Math Training Set Solutions – Data Sufficiency

‘

‘

Here are the five answer choices:

(1) Statement (1) alone is sufficient, but statement (2) alone is not sufficient

(2) Statement (2) alone is sufficient, but statement (1) alone is not sufficient

(3) Both statements TOGETHER are sufficient, but NEITHER statement ALONE is sufficient

(4) EACH statement ALONE is sufficient

(5) Statements (1) and (2) TOGETHER are NOT sufficient

1. The conditions together are sufficient, but neither alone is sufficient. Condition (1) gives the information about what the 3rd year associate charges, Condition (2) provides additional information about the amount that the 1st and the 2nd charge. The answer to the question is \$100. If the 1st year associate charges x, then the 2nd year associate charges $\frac{3}{2}x$, and the 3rd year associate charges twice as much, i.e. $3x$, which is given to be \$300. Hence $x = \frac{300}{3} = 100$ dollars. Therefore, the best answer is (C).

2. (1) provides dollar spending on the item which falls into Health and Fitness category. Since spas may not be the only item in Health and Fitness, we cannot calculate Michelle's total annual dollar spending. So, (1) is irrelevant to the main question in that (1) gives no information about the distribution of health and fitness spending on items other than spas. Whereas, from (2) it is clear that Michelle's total annual dollar spending is $\frac{100}{19} \times 20,000$, which means that her spending on clothes was $\frac{20}{19} \times 20,000$. Therefore, the best answer is (B).

3. The answer cannot be determined from the information given. The reason for it is that the intervals $(0, \frac{5}{6})$ and $(\frac{2}{3}[= \frac{4}{6}], 1)$ overlap. So, one can find a number v in the interval $(\frac{4}{6}, 1)$ such that $v > u$. Therefore, the best answer is (E).

4. Condition (2) gives the capacity of tanker R, which, when combined with the first sentence of the question, will give the capacity of Tanker S. Then, Condition (1) implies how much oil there are in each tanker at the moment. So, both conditions are needed. In what follows, all capacities are in thousands gallons of oil. The capacity of a sea-going tanker S is $\frac{40}{0.5} = 80$. Since R is 90 percent full, R's current load is $40 \times 0.9 = 36$. S is 40 percent full, so its current load is $80 \times 0.4 = 80 \times \frac{2}{5} = 32$. So, the difference required is $36 - 32 = 4$. Therefore, the best answer is (C).

5. (1) says that $-4q < 0$, so $q > 0$, and (2) implies the same thing; if $-q < 0$, then $q > 0$, and q is a positive number. Therefore, the best answer is (D).

6. Condition (2) is not sufficient since two equations cannot determine three unknowns uniquely.

   If 20 were indeed the average, then $\frac{u+v+w+20}{4} = 20$ would hold. If it were to hold, then $u + v + w = 4 \times 20 - 20 = 60$. This is exactly condition (1). Therefore, the best answer is (A).

7. Condition (2) implies Condition (1). Car Q covered the distance in 3 hours, and Car P completed the race in 40 minutes, which yields that car P was racing for 3 hours and 40 minutes in total. Translate 3 hours and 40 minutes into fractions: $3\frac{2}{3} = \frac{11}{3}$. The average speed of car P is $\frac{300}{\frac{11}{3}} = \frac{3 \times 300}{11} = \frac{900}{11} = 81\frac{9}{11}$. Therefore, the best answer is (D).

8. Each statement alone is sufficient. A function of the type $y = x^{\text{odd}}$ has the property, unlike the function of the type $u = v^{\text{even}}$, that for each number in the range of the function there exists a unique number in the domain. It is also strictly increasing. So, $p^3 > q^3$ unambiguously implies that $p > q$, whereas $u^2 > v^2$ may yield the values of u and v such that $u < v$. Suppose that $u^2 = 4, v^2 = 3$ and $u = -2 < \sqrt{3} = v$. Clearly, $p - q > 0$ implies that $p > q$. Therefore, the best answer is (D).

9. Each condition alone is sufficient. From (1), we can infer that 35 students make 35 percent of the students with another doctorate degree. From (2), we know that 45 students make 45 percent of the student body who have obtained a master's degree before being admitted to the doctoral program at the business school. Therefore, the best answer is (D).

10. A positive multiple of a Pythagorean triple is a Pythagorean triple. Condition (1) provides no information to answer the question. One can construct a triangle with side which do not form a Pythagorean triple such that its area is a multiple of the area of S. Therefore, the best answer is (B).

11. Conditions (1) and (2) together are not sufficient to produce a unique remainder of w. Suppose that $w = 30$, then w is a multiple of an odd integer, 5, and it is a multiple of 5. Here, the remainder is 0. If $w = 25$, then it is an odd multiple of 5, and the remainder is 1. Therefore, the best answer is (E).

12. The answer cannot be determined from the information given. One needs to know the total number of applicants either in 1999 or in 2003, or what fraction the increase of $20,000(2,000)$ applicants is of the number of applicants in 1999. Therefore, the best answer is (E).

13. It is given in the body of the question that the ship had arrived ahead of schedule. So, it is possible to construct two equations with two unknowns on the basis of condition (1) and the information given in the body of the question. Let e be earnings per day and δ be the number of days ahead of schedule. From the information given in the body of the question we have that $3,850 = 20e + 2\delta e$, and from condition (1) we have that $4,200 = 20e + (\delta + 1)2e$. $\delta = 1$ and $e = 175$ solves both equations. Condition (2) implies that $3,850 = 20 \cdot 175 + 2\delta \cdot 175$, for which $\delta = 1$ is a solution. Therefore, the best answer is (D).

14. Either condition may be used to answer the question. Since c is the cost of the first gadget, $(1/2)c$ is the cost of the second, and $(1/4)c$ is the cost of the third gadget, etc., the cost, c_n, of the nth gadget is

$$c_n = \frac{c}{2^{n-1}}.$$

From (1), $c_3 + c_4 = c/4 + c/8 = (3c/8) = 9$, and $c = 24$.

From (2), $c_2 + c_9 = c/2 + c/2^8 = \frac{c(2^7+1)}{2^8}$, and $c = 24$. Therefore, the best answer is (D).

15. Condition (2) is superfluous. If a number is divisible by 6, it is divisible by any prime number that 6 consists of. The only two-digit number with repeated digits, RR, which is divisible by 6 is 66. For $Q66$ to be divisible by 3, Q must be divisible by 3, whereas Q could be any number. Therefore, the best answer is (E). Another way you can test the divisibility of 3 is that the sum of $Q + 2R$ needs to be divisible by 3. To check, plug in $R = 6$ and $Q = 4$. For $Q = 4$, QRR is not divisible by 3. If you try $R = 6, Q = 6$, QRR is. Hence, (E) is correct.

16. The solution method makes clear that both conditions are necessary. If x is the number of passengers who boarded the flight at Arequipa, then the number of passengers arriving at Cuzco on the same flight equals the number of passengers on the plane when it left Lima minus those disembarked in Arequipa plus those who first boarded in Arequipa on the way to Cuzco, i.e. $163 = 184 - 30 + x, x = 9$. Therefore, the best answer is (C).

17. Condition (1) yields the angle measurements of the triangle. If x is a common multiple of angle measures, then we can conclude that the total measure of three angles is $6x$, and since angle measures of a triangle add up to $180°$, $6x = 180$, $x = 30$. So, two other angle measures are $60°$ and $90°$, it is a right triangle. In addition, it is a $30° - 60° - 90°$ triangle, in which the sides are related as $1 : \sqrt{3} : 2$. Then, it follows from (2) that the legs of the right triangle are of length 5 and $5\sqrt{3}$, and the area of the triangle is $\frac{25\sqrt{3}}{2}$. Therefore, the best answer is (C).

18. Condition (1) gives the retail price and Condition (2) gives the retailer's mark-up. Both are necessary to find out the wholesale price of a single t-shirt. If w is the wholesale price of a single t-shirt, then the retain price of \$4.80 is w plus a retail mark-up of 20 percent: $4.80 = w + \frac{20}{100}w = 1.2w$, $w = \frac{4.80}{1.2} = \frac{4.80}{\frac{6}{5}} = \frac{5}{6} \times 4.80 = 4$. Now, the lot of 25 t-shirts at wholesale price costs $4 \times 25 = 100$ dollars. Therefore, the best answer is (C).

19. Condition (1) forces each permutation to be only 4 characters long. What this monkey achieves, as Condition (2) states, is to create all possible distinct permutations of the keys that are functioning. If only 4 keys are functioning, and letters in each word are not repeated, then the total number of distinct permutations is $4 \times 3 \times 2 \times 1 = 24$. Therefore, the best answer is (C).

20. The answer cannot be determined from the information given. Condition 1 imply that $z = 3y$, where y is either odd or even. If y is odd, then $z = 3y$ is odd. If y is even, then z is even. Condition 2 implies that $z = 9y$, where y is either odd or even. If y is odd, then $z = 9y$ is odd. If y is even, then z is even. Therefore, the answer is (E).

21. Since $AC = 4$ and $\angle BAC = \angle ACD$, $\triangle ABC = \triangle CAD$. So, it is sufficient to find the area of just one of them.

From (1), it follows that $\triangle ABC$ is a right triangle since $4^2 = 2^2 + (2\sqrt{3})^2$, and its right angle is at the vertex B. So, the area of ABC is $2\sqrt{3}$, and the area of $ABCD$ is $4\sqrt{3}$.

From (2), $\triangle ABC$ is a $30° - 60° - 90°$ triangle itself with the right angle at the vertex B. Its sides are related as $1 : \sqrt{3} : 2$. So, AB is half the hypotenuse, i.e. $AB = 2$ and $BC = 2\sqrt{3}$, and the area of $\triangle ABC$ is $2\sqrt{3}$, and the area of $ABCD$ is twice the area of ABC. Therefore, the best answer is (D).

22. It is given that Q is a subset of integers, and 11 is in Q, i.e. 11 is an element of the set. Since 11 is in Q, we can say that it is a particular element of Q, so we can assume q equals a specific value. In this case, $q = 11$. So, if $q = 11$, then (1) implies that $q + 11 = 11 + 11 = 2 \cdot 11$ is also in Q. Now, it follows, since q denotes any generic element of Q, that $2 \cdot 11 + 11 = 3 \cdot 11$ is in Q. In this fashion we can continue ad infinitum: $3 \cdot 11, 4 \cdot 11, ...,$ etc. Hence, we conclude that any number of form $k \cdot 11$, where k is a positive integer, is in Q. This is the same as saying that Q contains only positive multiples of 11. Hence, (1) alone is sufficient, and the best answer is (A). Similar reasoning applied to (2) implies that Q contains only negative multiples of 11. For this property of generating an entire set, a number which plays a role of integer 11 in this problem is often termed to be the *generator* of the set.

23. For starters, it is easy to solve (2). Squaring both sides and rearranging terms, we can conclude that $q = 3$. Substituting this value of q into (1) does not lead to an equality: $(2 \cdot 3 - 3)^2 \neq 3$. So, answer (D) can be eliminated. (C) can also be eliminated since neither (1) nor (2) imply anything that can be used in the other condition to arrive at the unique value of q.

Now, we can solve the quadratic in (1) to see if it has distinct roots. $(2q - 3)^2 = q^2$ expands into

$$\begin{aligned} 4q^2 - 12q + 9 &= q^2, \\ 3q^2 - 12q + 9 &= 0. \end{aligned}$$

Since the quadratic is in standard form of $ax^2 + bx + c = 0$, its discriminant can be computed according to the standard formula The discriminant of this quadratic is

$$\begin{aligned} \mathcal{D} &= b^2 - 4 \cdot a \cdot c \\ &= 12^2 - 4 \cdot 3 \cdot 9 \\ &= 144 - 108 = 36 > 0. \end{aligned}$$

A non-zero $\mathcal{D}$ implies that the quadratic has two distinct roots which are different from the value of q implied by (2). Since only condition (2) implies a unique value of q, the best answer is (B).

24. If $ab > 0$, then either $a > 0$ and $b > 0$ or $a < 0$ and $b < 0$. Since $a^4 > 0$, both a and b are strictly positive, hence $a + b > 0$. Condition (2) implies that both a and b are of the same sign, which can lead to either a positive or a negative sign of

their sum. Therefore, the best answer is (A).

25. (1) implies two values of a different in sign. Therefore, $6a + b = 48$ will give two values of b. The equation in (2) and $6a + b = 48$ uniquely determine the values of a and b. Therefore, the best answer is (B).

26. In this problem, the total number of tickets to both finals is not relevant to the actual percentage of total tickets purchased. This is because that the ratio of the total number of tickets for men's final to the total number of tickets to women's final is already given as $3 : 2$. In condition (2), the percentages of tickets purchased for both men's and women's finals are also given. Combining the two, the percentage of total tickets purchased can be derived. The correct answer is (B).

Specifically, assume T to be the total number of tickets for both finals. Men's final ticket number is $3/5 \times T$. Women's final ticket number is $2/5 * T$. The total percentage of tickets purchased is: $(90\% \times 3/5 \times T + 80\% \times 2/5 \times T)/T$. That is 86%.

27. The answer cannot be obtained from the information given. Neither Condition (1) nor Condition (2) specifies total gross receipts at the box office in excess of the cost. Therefore, the best answer is (E).

28. Condition (1) is irrelevant since it has to do with the trading volume, which is just the number of shares changing hands. The ratio required is $\frac{6}{8} = \frac{3}{4}$. Therefore, the best answer is (B).

29. One need not know the number of guests since Condition (2) states that 20 kilos of dough is sufficient for a cake, which is big enough to leave none of the guests' sugar cravings unsatisfied. If a baker were to take, by weight, 3 units of water, 7 of flour, and 2 of yeast, then $\frac{3}{12}$ of the dour mixture would be water. So, to make 20 kilograms of dough, a baker needs $\frac{3}{12} \times 20 = \frac{3 \times 2 \times 2 \times 5}{2 \times 2 \times 3} = 5$ kilograms of water. Therefore, the best answer is (B).

30. Condition (1) is equivalent to $\frac{7}{u} = 14, u = \frac{7}{14} = \frac{1}{2}$. Condition (2) yields the same result. $2 = \frac{1}{u}$ implies that $u = \frac{1}{2}$. Therefore, the best answer is (D).

31. (1) alone implies that $v = 2$ or -2, which does not determine the value of the fraction uniquely. (2) and $u = v^4$ together state that $v^5 = 32$, $v = 2$. Hence, $\frac{v}{u} = \frac{2}{16} = \frac{1}{8} = 0.125$. Therefore, the best answer is (B).

32. Using (1), it is easy to construct an example of a parallelogram with equal diagonals in which all sides are equal in length, e.g. a square, or differ in length, e.g. a rectangular.

(2) implies that $\triangle CDF$ is equilateral, which in turn implies that all edges of $CDEF$ are the same since in any parallelogram the triangles, which share a diagonal, are equal. Therefore, the best answer is (B).

33. The area of any triangle is $\frac{bh}{2}$, where b and h are the lengths of the base and the altitude, respectively. So, knowing the length of either b or h and the relationship between them, one can determine the other lengths to answer the question. Therefore, the best answer is (C).

34. (1) implies that y is even, and (2) says that $2y$ is even, which is true for both even and odd integer y. Therefore, the best answer is (A).

35. If (1) alone is assumed, then either $x = 1$ or $x = -1$. If (2) is assumed, then $x = +\sqrt{-x}$ or $x = -\sqrt{-x}$, and the only real number which makes one of these possibilities true is -1. Therefore, the best answer is (B).

36. Vertices where transmitter, receiver, and the relay station are located form a right triangle. Condition (1) gives the length of the hypotenuse. Condition (2) gives the length of a leg opposite the vertex where the receiver is located, so the Pythagorean theorem gives the length of the leg. Since the speed of the signal is known and constant, one can compute relevant times and determine their difference. Therefore, the best answer is (C).

37. The answer cannot be determined from the information given. In order to determine which version of the drug yields a greater dollar profit to the pharmacy, you need to compare between dollar profits from the two versions. Hence, you need to compare the dollar profit per box and the number of boxes sold for each version. The problem itself reveals that the mark-up percentage for the patented is higher than the generic. Statement (1) shows that the cost per box for the patented version is higher than the generic. Therefore, you can conclude that the patented version generates more dollar profit per box than the generic. However, statement (2) never provides the missing information on the comparison of the number of boxes sold. Instead it only compares the two in terms of weight. The best answer is (E).

38. Condition (1) gives the definition of the operation denoted as $\triangle$. Condition (2) gives the values of x and y. So, the answer is clear without any calculations. The best answer is (C) since (1) provides the definition of the operation $\triangle$ and (2) provides the numerical values for the operands. Despite the fact that the computation is not necessary, we provide it anyway. Using the definition of $\triangle$ from (1) and Condition (2) for values of x and y, we have that

$$
\begin{aligned}
x \triangle y &= \frac{x^3}{y} + \frac{y^2}{x} \\
&= \frac{3^3}{5} + \frac{5^2}{3} \\
&= \frac{3 \cdot 9}{5} + \frac{25}{3} \\
&= \frac{9 \cdot 9}{15} + \frac{125}{15} \\
&= \frac{81 + 125}{15} = \frac{206}{15} \\
&= 13\frac{13}{15}.
\end{aligned}
$$

Therefore, the best answer is (C).

39. The time period U is just 3 minutes long, no matter what time measuring scheme, military or otherwise, is being used. So, it lasts only for 180 seconds. Therefore, the best answer is (D).

40. The answer cannot be determined from the information given. If h, w, and l are the height, width, and length of P, respectively, then the surface area $S = 2wl + 2wh + 2lh$. The volume V of P is equal to $wlh = 2wl = 24$ cubic meters, and $wl = 12$ sq. meters. So, it is impossible to determine wh and lh. Therefore, the best answer is (E).

41. In a triangle, the length of one side must be always strictly less than the sum of lengths of two other sides. Condition (1) gives the sum of length of u and v. Condition (2) gives just the length of u. Therefore, the best answer is (A).

42. Since $\triangle ABC$ and $\triangle EDC$ are $30° - 60° - 90°$ triangles, the distance that R covers on the first leg is twice the distance that S covers on the same leg. So, if it moves twice as fast, it will meet S at C and will continue along the edge CD with the same speed as S moved along the edge BC. Hence, the snails arrive at their respective destination simultaneously. Therefore, the best answer is (B).

43. (1) gives the difference in the draft numbers between the two countries. Since the difference of two numbers does not determine the numbers uniquely, knowing the difference is not sufficient to answer the question. (2) implies that the draft in country X was $5 \cdot 300,000$, and the draft in country Y was $10/3 \cdot 141,000$. So, the draft to the army of each country can be determined uniquely. Therefore, the best answer is (B).

44. We know that $P + O + R = Q + O + S$. Then we can reduce it to $P + R = Q + S$. From (1) $Q + R = 15$ and $S = 4$, we cannot derive the number for P. (2) does not add new information to the equation. So, P is not determined uniquely, and, therefore, the best answer is (E).

45. Let F denote total number of rowing team members enrolling as new fraternity members. Let R denote total number of rowing team members. (1) yields the fraternity's initial goal in terms of the number of the rowing team members. Based on the question and (1), we can conclude: $15\% \times R \times (1 + 20\%) = F$. (2) gives the value of F. $F = 40$. Therefore, the best answer is (C).

46. In Condition (1), we can conclude there are multiple prime numbers in the range such as 23, 29 and 31. In Condition (2), we can conclude there are even more prime numbers in the range including 19 and the three numbers above. So neither condition results in just a single prime number. When you consider both conditions, there are still three prime numbers left. So the answer is (E).

47. The answer to the question is 0. It is useful to know that $a^3 - b^3 = (a - b)(a^2 + ab + b^2)$. Therefore, the best answer is (A).

48. Condition (1) yields that $v < 0$ since an odd power of a negative number is negative, and an even power of any number is positive. Condition (2) yields that $u < 0$. So, it follows that $uv > 0$ since a product of two negative numbers is positive. Therefore, the best answer is (C).

49. The subset of real numbers divisible by 5 is countably infinite with no largest or smallest element. The greatest negative multiple of a prime number must be -2. Therefore, the best answer is (B).

50. Each condition alone is sufficient. Set $\frac{u}{v} = c$, then from (1), $c = 15$, and from (2), $c = 15$. Therefore, the best answer is (D).

51. The triangles in the figure are similar. Similarity implies that $\frac{AB}{GI} = \frac{BC}{HG}$, and from (2) $AB \cdot HG = BC \cdot GI = 24$. Therefore, the best answer is (B).

52. Since the set is inserted into the box in such a way that its longest dimension corresponds to the width of the box, the thickness of the set determines the number of sets per box. So, information in condition (2) is irrelevant to the question. Therefore, the best answer is (A).

53. If T, P, and J are the number of races that Tim, Pete, and John won, respectively. Then, Condition (1) states that $T = \frac{3}{7}P$, and Condition (2) states that $P = \frac{7}{3}J$. So, $T = \frac{3}{7} \times \frac{7}{3}J, T = J$. So, $P = \frac{7}{3}J = \frac{7}{3}T$. So, Pete won most of the races. Therefore, the best answer is (C).

54. The answer cannot be obtained from the information given. Condition (2) says nothing about the average salary of a professor at University D since the number of faculty at University D is not given. Therefore, the best answer is (E).

55. Condition (2) and the fact that July is 31 days long uniquely fix the schedule of the yacht club. It is an easy check that Friday and Sunday occur four times given (2). Condition (1) allows for three possibilities. Given (1), Tuesday may occur either on the first, or on the second, or on the third of July. If Tuesday occurs on the first of the month, then the last day of the month is a Thursday, a day with no race, and the total number of races in this case is 8. If Tuesday is the second of the month, then the last day of the month is a Wednesday with 8 races taking place. If Tuesday is the third of the month, then the first of the month is a Sunday, a race, and Tuesday is the last day of the month, with 9 races taking place. Therefore, the answers (A) and (D) can be eliminated. So, since (2) uniquely fixes the schedule of the races for the month of July, the best answer is (B).

56. (1) and (2) together imply that $PS = 4$ and the altitude of $PQRS$ is 2. Then, the total area of $PQRS$ can be expressed as a sum of a rectangle and two equal triangles. Therefore, the best answer is (C).

57. Multiply both sides of the equation in Condition (2) by 2 to obtain the equation in Condition (1). Therefore, the best answer is (D).

58. Condition (2) indicates τ can be 0. If we cancel τ on both sides of the equation in (1), we obtain a quadratic $(\tau - 1)^2 = 4$, which expands into the standard quadratic form $\tau^2 - 2\tau - 3 = 0$.

A quadratic $ax^2 + bx + c = 0$ has at most two roots and can be obtained via two methods. Having obtained the roots, one can factor the quadratic into the product

$$ax^2 + bx + c = (x + r_1)(x + r_2).$$

The general methods involve computing the discriminant $\mathcal{D}$. For the standard form quadratic $ax^2 + bx + c = 0$, the discriminant is given by the formula

$$\mathcal{D} = b^2 - 4ac.$$

Then, the roots are

$$r_1, r_2 = -\frac{-b \pm \sqrt{\mathcal{D}}}{2a}.$$

The second methods involves re-writing the standard form quadratic as $x^2 + \frac{b}{a}x + \frac{c}{a} = 0$. Then, notice that, since

$$x^2 + \frac{b}{a}x + \frac{c}{a} = (x + r_1)(x + r_2) = x^2 + (r_1 + r_2)x + r_1 r_2,$$

the sum of the roots must equal $-(b/a)$ and their product must equal c/a, i.e.

$$\begin{aligned} b/a &= r_1 + r_2, \\ c/a &= r_1 r_2 \end{aligned}$$

In this problem, the standard form quadratic is $\tau^2 - 2\tau - 3 = 0$.

$$\mathcal{D} = b^2 - 4ac = (2)^2 - 4 \cdot (-3) = 16 > 0,$$

so the roots are distinct, and the roots are given by

$$\frac{-b - \sqrt{\mathcal{D}}}{2a} = \frac{2 - 4}{2} = -1$$

and

$$\frac{-b + \sqrt{\mathcal{D}}}{2a} = \frac{2 + 4}{2} = 3.$$

The second method involves solving a system of equations

$$\begin{aligned} -2 &= r_1 + r_2, \text{and} \\ -3 &= r_1 r_2. \end{aligned}$$

So, the solution is −3 and 1. Since the value of τ obtained can be 0, −1 and 3. Therefore it is not unique, The best answer is (E).

59. From (1), both $\frac{3}{1} = 3$ and $3 \cdot 1 = 3$. From (2), both $\frac{0}{3} = 0$ and $0 \cdot 3 = 0$. Therefore, the best answer is (E).

60. The key is to realize that information related to the altitude of the pyramid is missing. So, it is impossible to compute the area of its lateral segments. Condition (1) states that each lateral triangle has a base length of 6 meters. Condition (2) implies that all lateral triangles are isosceles. Since the area of a triangle is a product of half the length of the height times the base, an additional piece of information is required. It may be the length of a perpendicular dropped onto the base, or the length of another side, or an angle measure. Therefore, the best answer is (E).

61. The triangle inequality states that the sum of any of its two sides is always greater than the third side. To obtain a bona fide triangle the phrase 'as least as big as' must be replaced with 'strictly greater than'. Condition (1) implies that $u + 5 = w < u + v$, and it follows that $v > 5$. Condition (2) again implies that v must exceed the value of 5. If $v \le 5$, then u and v are both contained in the line segment w. Therefore, the best answer is (D).

62. Both conditions provide for the unique answer of 42. From (1), the tens digit is twice the units digit or $t = 2u$, and from (2), the sum of both digits $t + u$ is 6. So, $u = 2$ and $t = 4$. Therefore, the best answer is (C).

63. The answer cannot be determined from the information given. If one were to use Condition (1) to answer the question, she would need to know the number of faculty members in the business school. In case of Condition (2), she would need to know the total number of clusters in the business school. Neither is provided by the conditions. Therefore, the best answer is (E).

64. The product of two odd numbers y is odd, and the sum of two odd numbers, $x + y^2$, is even. Therefore, the best answer is (C).

65. We need both conditions. Condition (1) implies that the product, rs, is even since any multiple of an even number is even. Condition (2) states that the value of $rs + t$ is either even or odd depending on the parity of t. t is a multiple of 3,

which can be both even, e.g. 6, and odd, e.g. 15. So, the parity of $rs + t$ cannot be determined uniquely. Therefore, the best answer is (E).

66. From (1), we can conclude that $ABCD$ is a rectangle, and from (2) we can conclude that $ABCD$ is a rectangle. This information is not sufficient to find the area of $ABCD$. To obtain the area of $ABCD$, we have to know either the length of any side of $ABCD$ or the measure of an angle between the diagonals of $ABCD$. This information is provided neither by (1) nor by (2). Therefore, the best answer is (E).

67. If c is the capacity of the reservoir in thousands of cubic meters of water, then Condition (1) states that $(3/4)c + 3,000 = (7/8)c$, and $c = 24,000$. Condition (2) states that $(3/4)c - 6,000 = (1/2)c$, and $c = 24,000$. Each of these equations provides the same value of c. Therefore, the best answer is (D).

68. $42 = 2 \times 3 \times 7$, and u cannot be a multiple of v^2 for any value of $v = 2, 3, 5, 7$, etc. The fact that v is a prime is given in the body of the question and not in the conditions. So, (2) alone is sufficient. Therefore, the best answer is (B).

69. Each condition yields an equation with two unknowns, the capacity of reservoir and its current level. Two equations with two unknowns give a unique solution.

Let c denote the capacity of the reservoir in thousand gallons and g be the amount of water the reservoir currently contains. In terms of this notation, Condition (1) states that $\frac{2}{3}g = \frac{1}{2}c$. Condition (2) states that $g + 60 = c$. From Condition (1), $c = \frac{4}{3}g$. Substituting this expression to Condition (2), we can obtain that $60 + g = \frac{4}{3}g$, and $\frac{1}{3}g = 60, g = 180$. Therefore, the best answer is (C).

70. Since neither u nor v is 0 as given by $uv \neq 0$, and the denominator is never zero, we can obtain the value of the fraction by using both conditions (1) and (2). The calculations become much easier if 27 is represented as a power of 3, i.e. $u = 27 = 3^3$. The expression above can be re-written as

$$\frac{3^4 \times (3^3)^3 - (3 \times 3^3)^3}{3^4 \times (3^3)^4} = \frac{3^{13} - 3^{12}}{3^{16}}$$

$$= \frac{3^{12}(3 - 1)}{3^{16}}$$

$$= \frac{2}{3^4} = \frac{2}{81}.$$

Therefore, the best answer is (C).

71. Both conditions imply that Bin had more money in his account than Joern had at the end of the year of travels. Since there were no additional deposits or withdrawals during the trip except the fixed monthly insurance payments, the relative relationship between the balance of Bin's and Joern's accounts remained constant. Therefore, the best answer is (D). If the question asked the difference in the balances at the end of the trip, then you would have to construct a system of equations to compute the initial amount of money in each account in the beginning of the year of travels. Let B denote the beginning balance of Bin's account, J denote the beginning balance of Joern's account. $B - -1200 = 2(J - 1200)$; $B - -1800 = 4(J - -1800)$. The result is $B = 3000$ and $J = 2100$.

72. Nothing is given about the distribution of scores across 30 games played. Team U could have won some games with a large score difference from Team R, but it also could have lost a majority of the games with a small advantage of Team R in those games. Therefore, the best answer is (E).

73. The key is to notice that the question asks about the fraction of labor to the total cost. The actual amounts are irrelevant to the question. Let l and e be the amounts paid for labor and equipment. From (2), we have that

$$e = \frac{5}{6}(l + e), \quad \frac{e}{e + l} = \frac{5}{6}, \quad \frac{l}{e + l} = 1 - \frac{5}{6} = \frac{1}{6}.$$

Therefore, the best answer is (B).

74. The answer cannot be determined from the information given. We are given the initial direction to the island, but we do not know the initial distance from the island to the airplane. On the basis of the information given, the island could be south-east of the airplane or north-east of the airplane. Therefore, the best answer is (E).

75. Condition (1) implies that $a \neq 0, b \neq 0$, and $a^2 = b^2$ by cross-multiplying. Expanding the quadratic in (2), we can obtain that

$$a^2 - 2ab + b^2 = a^2 - b^2, \quad 2b^2 - 2ab = 0.$$

Since $b \neq 0$, the second expression above simplifies to $2b - 2a = 0$, or $a = b$. Therefore, the best answer is (C).

76. One can construct two equations with two unknowns, where the unknowns are

the costs of toys, and each equation corresponds to a condition. They are $P + S = 40$, $P/S = 2/5$, and the values of P and S follow easily from them. Therefore, the best answer is (C).

77. The values of p, q, r, and s could be $1, 1, 1$, and 5, respectively, instead of $2, 2, 2$, and 2. Therefore, the best answer is (E).

78. First notice that a large triangle with side T is obtained from putting together four small triangles with side t. So, it follows that $T = 2t$. Also, recall that the sides of $30° - 60° - 90°$ triangles are related as $1 : \sqrt{3} : 2$. So, the altitude of the T-triangle is $\sqrt{3}T/2 = \sqrt{3}t$.

From (1), the area of the large triangle follows from the fact that $T = 2t$, and the area, A, of the triangle with side T (T-triangle) is

$$A = \frac{1}{2} \cdot T \cdot \frac{\sqrt{3}}{2} T = \frac{\sqrt{3}}{4} \cdot T^2 = \sqrt{3}t^2 = 144\sqrt{3}.$$

It follows from the fact that the altitude of T-triangle forms two $30° - 60° - 90°$ triangles with base $T/2$.

From (2), it is possible to determine the area of the small triangle (t-triangle) since the radii drawn from the center of the circle to vertices of t-triangle divide the triangle into three equal triangles. From one of this triangles, t is easily computed. See the figure below.

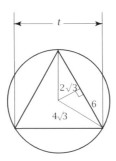

Again, we have used the property of $30° - 60° - 90°$ triangles that the lengths of their sides are related as $1 : \sqrt{3} : 2$. The triangle whose lengths are marked is a $30° - 60° - 90°$ triangle. Its hypotenuse (the radius of the circle) is $4\sqrt{3}$ in length. Its legs are $2\sqrt{3}$ and 6 units of length, respectively. So, it follows that $t/2 = 6$, $t = 12$, which is identical to condition (1). Therefore, the best answer is (D).

79. From (2), we can infer the equality of triangles, and (1) implies the measurements of the base and the height. Therefore, the best answer is (C).

80. The expression in Condition (1) lacks the variable c in the product, hence we cannot evaluate any multiple of abc on the basis of (1) alone. Therefore, the best answer is (B).

81. To answer the question, one needs to know not only the sign of even-numbered terms in the product but also the sign of odd-numbered terms in the product. Therefore, the best answer is (C).

82. Condition (2) only is sufficient. The caveat for this question is that 230 students who graduated last year were part of the graduate student body of 1120 students enrolled at various graduate programs. So, 230 need not be subtracted from 1120. The body of the question states the graduate school enjoys a $6\frac{1}{4}$ increase in enrollment over the previous year. So, this year's enrollment is

$$
\begin{aligned}
1120\left(1 + \frac{6\frac{1}{4}}{100}\right) &= 1120\left(1 + \frac{12\frac{1}{2}}{2 \times 100}\right) \\
&= 1120\left(\frac{2}{2} + \frac{0.125}{2}\right) \\
&= \frac{1120}{2} \times 2.125 \\
&= 1120 + \frac{560}{8} \\
&= 1120 + 70 = 1190.
\end{aligned}
$$

Therefore, the best answer is (B).

83. Condition (1) is irrelevant. Condition (2) states that 7 out of every 20 employees in the legal personnel are patent evaluators, or that the fraction of patent evaluators in the legal personnel is $\frac{7}{20}$. Hence, patent evaluators constitute $\frac{7}{20} \times 100 = 35$ percent of the firm's legal personnel. Therefore, the best answer is (B).

84. Given the first term, Condition (1), one can obtain the fourth term of the sequence. And, given the last term, one can obtain all the terms of the sequence by taking square roots sequentially. Clearly, the catch of the problem is that decomposing numbers into multiple of other numbers is harder that raising a number to the second power. So, it is not an easy guess that $81 = \sqrt{6561}$.

Given that the first term is 3, then the members of the sequence up to the fourth term are $3, 9, 81$, and 6561, which is the last term according to Condition (1). Therefore, either statement is sufficient. The best answer is (B).

85. From (1), one can determine that the length of a side of the triangle is 2 and obtain the altitude from considering the side lengths' of a $30° - 60° - 90°$ triangle. Condition (2) is irrelevant. Therefore, the best answer is (A).

86. One the basis of (1) alone, it is impossible to infer the speed of the fly revolving around O_2. Moreover, since the ratio of speeds is equal to the ratio of distances covered during one revolution, (2) alone is sufficient to answer the question. Therefore, the best answer is (B).

87. Although Condition (1) gives the total number of women in the trial, neither condition gives the total number of women who exhibited a reaction according to the pattern A. Therefore, the best answer is (E).

88. It does not matter how much of Cape Driver there is by volume or by mass. Since the alcohol content per unit of volume or mass is uniform, we can assign any volume or mass to the original components to derive the alcohol content of Cape Driver. Therefore, the best answer is (A).

89. The two conditions together are not sufficient. Suppose that the top and the bottom faces of the block B are squares with a side of length 2. Then, the height of the block is of length $4 = 64/16$, i.e. B is not a cube. Therefore, the best answer is (E).

90. Condition (1) alone is not sufficient since one of the competitors may earn most of the points and lose the final by losing in four or more events. Condition (2) indicates that one of the competitors won four events in a row. Nevertheless, it is not sufficient to determine that A won the final since B may win more events in the beginning but earn fewer points in later lost events. Therefore, the best answer is (E).

91. The key ideas of this question are the following:

The relationship of u^3 and u:

(1) When $u > 1$, $u^3 > u$

(2) When $0 < u < 1$, $u^3 < u$

The relationship of $u^{1/3}$ and u:

(1) When $u > 1$, $u^{1/3} < u$

(2)   When $0 < u < 1$, $u^{1/3} > u$

Condition (1) gives $u^3 < v$. Condition (2) gives $u^{1/3} < v$. Given what we learned above, we know that condition (1) and (2) both can have two scenarios: u and v are greater than 1 or less than 1. So either condition yields two possible results and does not lead to a final relation between u and v. However, if we combine the two conditions, we can get:

When v is greater than 1, regardless u is greater than 1 or between 0 and 1:

$u^3 < v \rightarrow u < v$

$u^{1/3} < v \rightarrow u$ can be greater than v or less than v.

So together, $u < v$.

When v is between 0 and 1:

$u^3 < v \rightarrow u$ can be greater than v or less than v and u has to be between 0 and 1 as well.

$u^{1/3} < v \rightarrow u < v$

So together, $u < v$.

You can also use some numbers to test out.

For example,

Condition 1 can yield: $2^3 < 9$ and $(1/2)^3 < (1/3)$. So no conclusion about the relation between u and v.

Condition 2 can yield: $(1/27)^{1/3} < (1/2)$ and $9^{1/3} < 5$. So no conclusion about the relation between u and v.

Then test out both conditions:

$2^3 < 9$ and $2^{1/3} < 9$. Conclusive.

$(1/27)^3 < (1/2)$ and $(1/27)^{1/3} < (1/2)$. Conclusive.

Another way to solve it is to draw it on a coordinate plane. Suppose that u belongs to the horizontal axis, and v belongs to the vertical axis. The collection of points on the plane, which satisfies Condition (1), is located between the vertical axis and the graph of the equation $v = u^3$. This area contains points located above and below 45°-line, so Condition (1) is insufficient to answer the question. The collection of points in the plane satisfying Condition (2) is located in quadrant I above the graph of the function $v = u^{1/3}$. These graphs intersect at the point $(1, 1)$ of the plane, and superimposing collections of points satisfying both Condition (1) and Condition (2) exclude the part of Quadrant I, which is below the 45°-line.

This shows that if u and v both satisfy (1) and (2), $v > u$ or vice versa depending on the letter labeling each axis.

Therefore, the best answer is (C).

92. Neither (1) nor (2) is sufficient. Since we do not know what other types of literature, e.g. poetry, historical accounts, etc., were there in the 28 books that Mary bought, we cannot determine the number of non-fiction books that Mary bought. Clearly, (1) is not sufficient. (2) does not provide any information on the number of non-fiction books. Therefore, the best answer is (E).

93. Condition (1) postulates an assumption that the GDP growth rate is constant over this 3-year period. Condition (2) gives numerical values.

    Let P_1, P_2, and P_3 denote the GDP for Country U during the years $1, 2$, and 3, respectively. Let r be the rate of growth. The condition (1) gives two equations: $P_2 = rP_1$, and $P_3 = rP_2$. Substituting the first one into the second, we obtain a relation between P_3 and P_1: $P_3 = r^2 P_1$, or $r = \sqrt{\frac{P_3}{P_1}}$. $\frac{P_3}{P_1} = \frac{338.4}{235} = 1.44$. So, $r = \sqrt{1.44} = 1.2$. This means that the rate of GDP growth of Country U was 20 percent.

    Therefore, the best answer is (C).

94. $CD = DF$ implies that $\triangle CDF$ is an isosceles, and so its angles at the base are of equal measure. So, given (2), $z = 180° - x = 180° - 120° = 60°$, and given (1), $z = 90 - y = 60°$. Therefore, the best answer is (D).

95. From (1), there are $27 + 21 - 30 = 18$ cars, which have a converter on both the engine and the exhaust pipes. Since 27 cars have more than one converters, one of which is attached to the engine, $27 - 18 = 9$ cars have just one converter attached to the engine only. It is impossible to infer from (2) how many cars have both converters. Therefore, the answer is (A).

96. Condition (1) is insufficient since it does not give the number of chips of each type. (2) yields two equations: $s + l = 512$, $s = 8l$, from which the values of s and l can be easily determined. Here, s is the number of 256-MB chips and l is the number of 512-MB chips. Therefore, the best answer is (B).

97. Condition (1) implies that the price of a bottle of Spanish wine, P_S equals $1.3P_I$. And Condition (2) states that the volume of a bottle of Spanish wine V_S equals

$1.25V_I$. So, we can determine the relationship between the price per unit volume of the two wines. Therefore, the best answer is (C).

98. The conditions together imply that the circle is inscribed into the square. Hence, the edge of the square is of length 32, and the perimeter of the square is 4×32. Therefore, the best answer is (C).

99. There are two cases. Either $XZ = ZY = 24$ or $XZ = 24, XY = YZ = 18$. Each case will give a different area. Therefore, the best answer is (E).

100. $12 = 40 + 32 - 60$ students were charged with both reckless driving and speeding. So, (2) is sufficient alone. Therefore, the best answer is (B).

101. There are two ways to solve the problem. One uses condition (1), the other uses condition (2). Using Condition (1) and the relation, we can obtain the height of the solid h: $\frac{8}{h} = \frac{4}{7}, h = 14$. Then, the surface area equals $2 \times 6 \times 8 + 2 \times 6 \times 14 + 2 \times 8 \times 14 = 448$. Differently, the relation $3 : 4 : 7$ means that width, length, and height have a common multiple, say, x. Then, the volume of the solid V is $V = 3 \times 4 \times 7x^3, x^3 = 8, x = 2$. So, the height h is 14. Therefore, the best answer is (D).

102. Condition (1) and (2) both imply the same thing: $z \leq 4$. So, the value of z may be $1, 2, 3$ or 4. Knowing this is not sufficient to answer the question conclusively.

     The question asks whether z may or may not be a prime number. Above, it is shown that z can be both. Therefore, the best answer is (E).

103. Let O be the point of intersection of AC and BD. Then (1) and (2) imply that $\triangle ABO = \triangle CDO$, which in turn implies that quadrilateral $ABCD$ is a parallelogram. Hence, R_1 and R_2 bisect angles of equal measure with a common edge, so they are parallel. Note that statement (1) alone is insufficient since it just indicates that the length of AB equals to that of DC. It can not be inferred that $AB//CD$. Statement (2) alone cannot support $AB//CD$ either. Therefore, the best answer is (C).

104. The body of the question says that $PQRS$ is a parallelogram. From (1), the area of $PQRS$ is the sum of areas of two equal equilateral triangles QRS and SQP, which area can be determined from $QS = 8$. (2) implies nothing about the height of $\triangle QRS$, only that $\triangle QRS$ is an isosceles. Therefore, the best answer is (A).

105.   It is possible to find a location of three points on a plane denoted as town, I_1, and I_2 in case when the town is closer to I_1 than to I_2, and vice versa. We also may need to assume that the ferry's speed is the same for both islands. Therefore, the best answer is (E).

106.   Since the requirement is to divide the pool into 20 equal sections, if one of the dimensions is 15 meters, then the only way to obtain 20 sections is to take 15 meters five times along the width of 75 meters divide the length of 100 meters in four pieces. Hence, under this division the dimensions are 15×25. From (2), the dimensions are the same, since it is impossible to obtain 20 pool sections if 75 meters is divided into three 25-meter sections. Therefore, the best answer is (D).

107.   Condition (2) provides the average for the whole trip, and one can infer only the total distance covered. (1) states that the hikers covered 260.5 miles during the first 10 days. So, the average was 26.05 miles per day. Therefore, the best answer is (A).

108.   The answer cannot be determined from the information given. 37 is an odd number with the properties stated in conditions (1) and (2). 72 is an even number with the same properties. Therefore, the best answer is (E).

109.   Condition (1) is irrelevant to the question. \$1.00 can buy $\frac{1}{0.25} = 4$ kilograms of oranges. Since the question requires the maximum amount of orange juice, we can assume that each kilogram of oranges yields 300 milliliters of juice. So, we can get $4 \times 300 = 1,200$ milliliters or 1.2 liters of juice. Therefore, the best answer is (B).

110.   If N is the number of items in the box, then (1) implies that $N = 3x + 2$, and for $x = 20, 21$, $N = 62, 65 < 70$. So, (1) does not determine N uniquely. From (2), $N = 9y + 2$, and for only one value of $y = 7$, $N = 65$. If $y = 6$, than $N = 56 < 60$; if $y = 8$, than $N = 74 > 70$. Therefore, the best answer is (B).

111. $u^3 = 64$ if, and only if $u = 4$. (1) and (2) together do not imply that $u = 4$. Therefore, the best answer is (E).

112.   (1) implies that four triangles AOB, COD, EOF, and GOH are equilateral with the side equal to 12. The other four triangles, the ones located between those mentioned above, are isosceles. Their area can be computed since the central angle (the angle from the center of the circle) is 30°. Therefore, the best answer is (A).

113. Condition (2) is insufficient since the number of parts of fat that the grain contains is not given. Instead, Condition (1) is enough. By weight, fats are $1 - \frac{5}{11} - \frac{7}{22} = \frac{22}{22} - \frac{17}{22} = \frac{5}{22}$ of the total mass of the grain. So, 66 pounds of the grains contains $\frac{5}{22} \times 66 = 5 \times 3 = 15$ pounds of fat. Therefore, the best answer is (A).

114. Both (1) and (2) imply that $PQRS$ is a parallelogram. The parallel sides of a parallelogram are equal, so $PQ = RS$. Therefore, the best answer is (C).

115. Condition (2) implies that $u = \frac{1}{2}$ or $u = -\frac{1}{2}$. From (1), $0 < u < u^{\frac{1}{3}} < 1$. Therefore, the best answer is (A).

116. Since the interview and hiring rates are not necessarily uniform for both nurses and doctors, (1) and (2) are insufficient to obtain an answer. Therefore, the best answer is (E).

117. The average speed at which Sasha drove was $\frac{240}{4} = 60$ miles per hour. Condition (1) is irrelevant. Therefore, the best answer is (B).

118. Condition (1) implies that $\frac{u}{4} = 11m$ and $\frac{v}{4} = 11n$ for $m, n < 11$ and $m \neq n$. So, $u = 44m$ and $v = 44n$, and 44 is the greatest common factor of u and v since $m, n < 11 < 44$. Therefore, the best answer is (A).

119. From (1), $v/u = 1/3$. Condition (2) yields that $\frac{72-u}{u}$ is v as a fraction of u, which cannot be determined precisely. Therefore, the best answer is (A).

120. Solving this question is equivalent to finding the area of one of the 8 equal triangles comprising a regular octagon. A triangle is solved completely if all measures of its angles and all lengths of its sides are known. To find this information, it is necessary and sufficient to know just three measures of a triangle in any of the following combinations, i.e. three angles, three sides, angle-angle-side, side-angle-side. One can see that this information can be obtained from Conditions (1) and (2) separately and the geometric properties of a regular octagon. Therefore, the best answer is (D).

121. The value of r is 1. To obtain r, we have to form the ratio of A and C and equate

the result to the value of the same ratio given in (1). The value of A is given, and $C = 2\pi r$.

$$\frac{A}{C} = \frac{\frac{3\sqrt{3}}{4}r^2}{2\pi r}$$
$$= \frac{3\sqrt{3}r}{8\pi} = \frac{8\pi}{3\sqrt{3}},$$

where the last fraction in the second line is given in (1). It is clear that the only value of r that maintains the second equality in the second line is that of $r = 1$. Since (2) is irrelevant, the best answer is (A).

122. Condition (1) implies that $y^2 - 5y + 6 = (y-2)(y-3)$, condition (2) implies that $y^2 - 7y + 12 = (y-3)(y-4)$. Since quadratics in (1) and (2) have a common root, the value of y that satisfies both (1) and (2) is determined uniquely. Therefore, the best answer is (C).

123. Knowing the perimeter of one of the pulleys, one can calculate the total distance drawn by the pulley. This distance is the same for the other pulley, and the ratio of the distance to the perimeter is the number of revolutions per unit time. Therefore, the best answer is (B).

124. Condition (2) implies that Pete completed 24 kilometers in the first two hours of his marathon. So, his average speed was 12 kilometers per hour. Therefore, the best answer is (C).

Chapter 5

Math Training Sets – Answer Keys

5.1 Problem Solving

(1) C

(2) C

(3) B

(4) A

(5) B

(6) C

(7) C

(8) D

(9) D

(10) D

(11) B

(12) B

(13) A

(14) B

(15) D

(16) A

(17) D

(18) D

(19) C

(20) E

(21) D

(22) C

(23) C

(24) E

(25) E

(26) E

(27) D

(28) C

(29) B

(30) E

(31) B

(32) B

(33) A

(34) A

(35) B

(36) B

(37) C

(38) D

(39) D

(40) D

(41) E

(42) B

(43) C

(44) E

(45) A

(46) D

(47) C

(48) E

(49) A

(50) D

(51) C

(52) E

(53) C

(54) D

(55) C

(56) D

(57) C

(58) E

(59) A

(60) C

(61) E

(62) E

(63) B

(64) B

(65) D

(66) C

(67) E

(68) C

(69) B

(70) C

(71) D

(72) B

(73) D

(74) E

(75) E

(76) C

(77) D

(78) B

(79) C

(80) D

(81) A

(82) A

(83) A

(84) A

(85) A

(86) C

(87) E

(88) D

(89) A

(90) D

(91) D

(92) D

(93) E

(94) D

(95) D

(96) C

(97) C

(98) A

(99) C

(100) C

(101) C

(102) A

(103) E	(127) B
(104) E	(128) D
(105) C	(129) D
(106) D	(130) B
(107) C	(131) C
(108) A	(132) E
(109) B	(133) B
(110) B	(134) B
(111) B	(135) C
(112) B	(136) D
(113) C	(137) C
(114) D	(138) B
(115) C	(139) D
(116) C	(140) A
(117) E	(141) D
(118) D	(142) C
(119) D	(143) E
(120) C	(144) C
(121) A	(145) E
(122) E	(146) A
(123) B	(147) B
(124) D	(148) D
(125) E	(149) C
(126) B	(150) C

5.2 Data Sufficiency

(1) C		(25) B	
(2) B		(26) B	
(3) E		(27) E	
(4) C		(28) B	
(5) D		(29) B	
(6) A		(30) D	
(7) D		(31) B	
(8) D		(32) B	
(9) D		(33) C	
(10) B		(34) A	
(11) E		(35) B	
(12) E		(36) C	
(13) D		(37) E	
(14) D		(38) C	
(15) E		(39) D	
(16) C		(40) E	
(17) C		(41) A	
(18) C		(42) B	
(19) C		(43) B	
(20) E		(44) E	
(21) D		(45) C	
(22) A		(46) E	
(23) B		(47) A	
(24) A		(48) C	
		(49) B	
		(50) D	

(51) B	(76) C
(52) A	(77) E
(53) C	(78) D
(54) E	(79) C
(55) B	(80) B
(56) C —	(81) C
(57) D	(82) B
(58) E	(83) B
(59) E	(84) D
(60) E	(85) A
(61) D	(86) B
(62) C	(87) E
(63) E	(88) A
(64) C	(89) E
(65) E	(90) E
(66) E	(91) C
(67) D	(92) E
(68) B	(93) C
(69) C	(94) D
(70) C	(95) A
(71) D	(96) B
(72) E	(97) C
(73) B	(98) C
(74) E	(99) E
(75) C	(100) B
	(101) D
	(102) E

(103) C	(114) C
(104) A	(115) A
(105) E	(116) E
(106) D	(117) B
(107) A	(118) A
(108) E	(119) A
(109) B	(120) D
(110) B	(121) A
(111) E	(122) C
(112) A	(123) B
(113) A	(124) C

Made in the USA
Charleston, SC
08 May 2014